Acre 1291

Bloody sunset of the Crusader states

Campaign · 154

OSPREY
PUBLISHING

Acre 1291

Bloody sunset of the Crusader states

David Nicolle · Illustrated by Graham Turner

Series editor Lee Johnson

First published in 2005 by Osprey Publishing
Midland House, West Way, Botley, Oxford OX2 0PH, UK
443 Park Avenue South, New York, NY 10016, USA
E-mail: info@ospreypublishing.com

A CIP catalogue record for this book is available from the British Library.

ISBN 1 84176 862 6

David Nicolle has asserted his right under the Copyright, Designs and Patents Act, 1988, to be identified as the Author of this Work

Editor: Alexander Stilwell
Design: The Black Spot
Index by Alison Worthington
Maps by The Map Studio
3D bird's-eye views by The Black Spot
Battlescene artwork by Graham Turner
Originated by Grasmere Digital Imaging, Leeds, UK
Printed in China through World Print Ltd.

05 06 07 08 09   10 9 8 7 6 5 4 3 2 1

For a catalogue of all books published by Osprey please contact:

NORTH AMERICA
Osprey Direct, 2427 Bond Street, University Park, IL 60466, USA
E-mail: info@ospreydirectusa.com

ALL OTHER REGIONS
Osprey Direct UK, P.O. Box 140, Wellingborough, Northants, NN8 2FA, UK
E-mail: info@ospreydirect.co.uk

www.ospreypublishing.com

Dedication

For Bob and Helen Rankin, almost 24/7

Key to military symbols

Army Group	Army	Corps	Division	Brigade	Regiment	Battalion
XXXXX	XXXX	XXX	XX	X	III	II

Company/Battery	Infantry	Artillery	Cavalry
I		•	

Key to unit identification

Unit identifier / Parent unit
Commander
(+) with added elements
(−) less elements

CONTENTS

GEOPOLITICAL LANDSCAPE

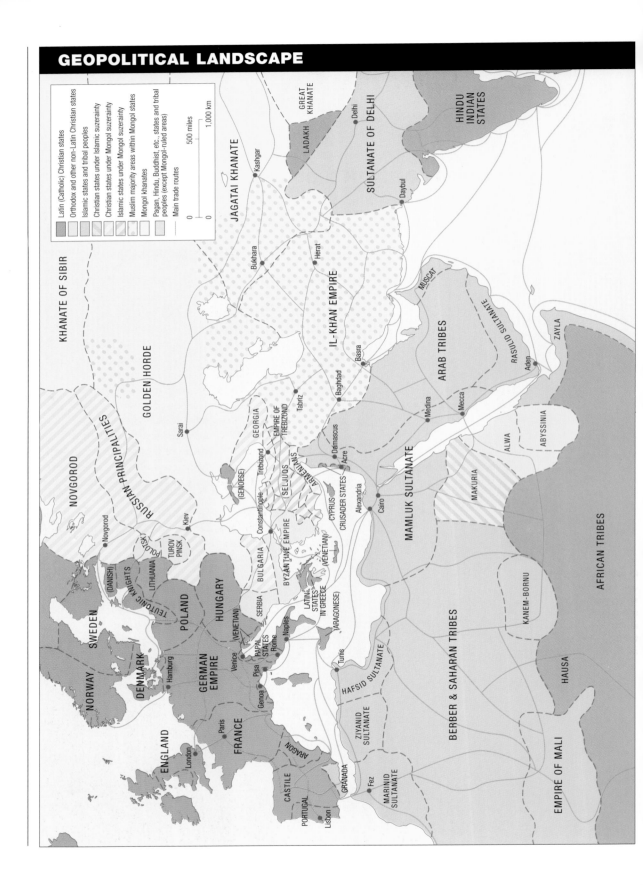

Latin (Catholic) Christian states
Orthodox and other non-Latin Christian states
Islamic states and tribal peoples
Christian states under Islamic suzerainty
Christian states under Mongol suzerainty
Islamic states under Mongol suzerainty
Muslim majority areas within Mongol states
Mongol khanates
Pagan, Hindu, Buddhist, etc. states and tribal
peoples (except Mongol-ruled areas)
Main trade routes

0   500 miles
0   1,000 km

KHANATE OF SIBIR

NOVGOROD

RUSSIAN PRINCIPALITIES

GOLDEN HORDE

JAGATAI KHANATE

GREAT
KHANATE

LADAKH

HINDU
INDIAN
STATES

SULTANATE OF DELHI

Delhi

Daybul

Kashgar

Bukhara

Herat

IL-KHAN EMPIRE

Basra

Baghdad

Tabriz

EMPIRE OF
TREBIZOND

GEORGIA

Trebizond

Sarai

Novgorod

Kiev

POLOSK

TUROV
PINSK

LITHUANIA

(DANISH)

TEUTONIC KNIGHTS

SWEDEN

NORWAY

DENMARK

Hamburg

GERMAN
EMPIRE

POLAND

HUNGARY

SERBIA

BULGARIA

(VENETIAN)

Venice

PAPAL
STATES

Rome

Naples

Pisa

Genoa

ENGLAND

London

FRANCE

Paris

ARAGON

CASTILE

PORTUGAL

Lisbon

GRANADA

Fez

MARINID
SULTANATE

ZIYANID
SULTANATE

HAFSID SULTANATE

Tunis

(ARAGONESE)

LATIN
STATES
IN GREECE

BYZANTINE EMPIRE

Constantinople

SELJUQS

ARMENIANS

CYPRUS

CRUSADER STATES

Acre

Damascus

Alexandria

Cairo

MAMLUK SULTANATE

Medina

Mecca

ARAB TRIBES

MUSCAT

RASULID SULTANATE

Aden

ZAYLA

ABYSSINIA

ALWA

MAKURIA

BERBER & SAHARAN TRIBES

KANEM-BORNU

HAUSA

EMPIRE OF MALI

AFRICAN TRIBES

(GENOESE)

THE ORIGINS OF THE CAMPAIGN

The fall of Acre in 1291 is seen by most western historians as a very significant event, and as the final chapter of the Crusading epic. It clearly had a huge psychological impact, but when compared to contemporary events in the wider Islamic world and in Europe, its geopolitical importance was small. Another 'problem' as far as European historians have been concerned is that the victors were of slave origin, and westerners have traditionally found 'rule by slaves' deeply abhorrent. Paradoxically, Middle Eastern scholars have been less concerned about this fact, recognizing that adult Mamluks were actually 'freed men' rather than slaves, and that the nobility or otherwise of a medieval Islamic ruler reflected his actions and piety rather than his origins. Until recently the aristocratically dominated societies of Europe also saw the rapid political changes which characterised the Mamluk Sultanate as evidence of a corrupt political system dominated by intrigue and assassination. In reality the Mamluk Sultanate was highly competitive, with power and legitimacy as prizes to be won by the strongest or cleverest.

Another paradox can be seen in the unexpected attitude towards Islam of some Christian thinkers around the time of the fall of Acre. Such scholars and missionaries maintained that Muslim beliefs were so close to Christianity that conversion should be easy. One such optimist was a Dominican friar, William of Tripoli, who lived in Acre and completed his book *On the State of the Saracens* in 1273. The great Italian poet Dante grew up while Acre was still in Crusader hands. He placed Saladin and other 'good Saracens' in Limbo in his *Divine Comedy*; not a place of torment but

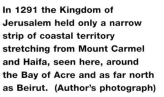

In 1291 the Kingdom of Jerusalem held only a narrow strip of coastal territory stretching from Mount Carmel and Haifa, seen here, around the Bay of Acre and as far north as Beirut. (Author's photograph)

containing 'a noble castle, defended with seven high walls, and moated round with a little river'. What these men failed to note was that similarity could be a two-way street, and the following centuries saw far greater conversion of Christians to Islam than vice-versa.

The Crusader States had been in steep though not uninterrupted decline during the 13th century and the Crusader King of Jerusalem was now called the King of Acre by Muslim chroniclers since losing his nominal capital in 1244. But even though the Kingdom of Jerusalem now consisted of no more than a narrow coastal strip from Acre to Beirut, it remained rich and the annual revenues of mid-13th century Acre alone were greater than the normal revenues of the King of England. Acre was still one of the most important ports in the eastern Mediterranean, and the Arab geographer al-Dimashki described it as it had been when he was young; 'Acre is a beautiful city. The people have their drinking water from an underground channel which comes into the town. There is a fine and spacious port, and artisans are numerous there.' Acre was also strong in defensive terms with a garrison ranging from the dedicated Military Orders to those mercenaries and militiamen whom Italian cities provided in return for commercial privileges.

The remaining Crusader mainland territories were now tiny enclaves almost wholly dependent upon maritime communications to provide them with food, munitions, troops and indeed their reason for existence, which remained trade between the Middle East and Europe. Meanwhile the Kingdom of Cyprus, though itself relatively weak, had a powerful economic interest in defending the mainland where Cypriot forces were often involved, though more usually in the civil wars than in defence against Mamluk attack.

The most important defenders of Acre were the Military Orders and, given the fanaticism of such men, it is surprising to note the Templars' association with the cult of Our Lady of Saidnaya in a mountain monastery near Damascus. Brethren went there to collect holy oil for Templar churches in Europe, though this might also have provided an opportunity for intelligence gathering inside Mamluk territory. On the other side, Acre was included in an early 13th century list of Islamic holy sites because it housed the Tomb of the pre-Islamic prophet Salih in what was at the time the Cathedral. And just inside the eastern city wall was the spring where an ox appeared, to help Adam till his fields after

None of Crusader Acre's urban towers survive, but they would have been similar to those in Italian cities, as shown in this stylized carving of an Italian urban *torre*. (*In situ* cemetery of the Abbey of Chiaravalle, Italy)

Acre's harbour defences were similar to those of Pisa, as illustrated in a late 13th-century carved relief. (Museo di Sant'Agostino, Genoa, Italy)

Members of the ruling Lusignan family of both Cyprus and Acre on a late 13th-century effigial slab from the Cathedral of Famagusta. (Limasol Museum, Cyprus)

being expelled from Paradise. Another vital military unit was the French Regiment of 100 knights plus crossbowmen which King Louis IX left in Acre in 1254. Thereafter French support for the Crusader Kingdom remained important and strong.

As Crusader territory gradually fell to Mamluk reconquest, many settler families realized they had no future in the area. Although only those with money for passage aboard a ship could leave, they included merchant families and prosperous peasants as well as the aristocracy. Many peasants apparently went to northern Italy – just those areas where most recruits would be found for the last disastrous Crusade of 1290. The situation may have been better around Tripoli which was separated from the great Islamic inland cities by Mount Lebanon, the indigenous inhabitants of which included Maronite Christians and Shi'a Muslims. These *jabaliyun* or mountain people were largely independent of both the Crusader County of Tripoli and the Mamluk Sultanate to the east, though at times they recognized the suzerainty of the Crusader Lords of Jubayl (Gibelet).

In Acre there was no longer a king in residence and the throne had been disputed between the Lusignan rulers of Cyprus and Princess Mary of Antioch. In 1277 she sold her claim to King Charles I of Naples, a member of the hugely powerful Angevin family – known in England as the Plantagenets – who was carving out a Mediterranean empire in Italy, Sicily, Greece and Albania. While Acre, Sidon and the Templars normally supported the Angevins, Tyre, Beirut and the Hospitallers supported the Lusignans. But then came the Sicilian Vespers revolt, a bitter war between the Angevins and the Aragonese from Spain for control of this area, followed by the death of King Charles, which combined to destroy Angevin ambitions in the east.

The Mongol invasions of the Middle East in the first half of the 13th century had a shattering impact upon the Islamic world, not only in the damage caused and casualties inflicted, but also in cultural and psychological terms. A civilization which had for centuries been the most

'St Nicholas calms the waves' on a Bulgarian wall-painting made in 1259. The art is Orthodox Christian but the ship and its crew are typically Western. (*In situ* Boyana Church, Sofia, Bulgaria)

creative in the world turned in upon itself, becoming conservative and defensive. The Mamluk Sultanate, which replaced the easygoing Ayyubid sultanates of Egypt and Syria, halted the Mongol advance but at a high price. The Mamluks would become great patrons of art, literature and architecture, but their state now became the servant of their army while professional soldiers – the Mamluks – formed the rulers and filled almost every office of state.

Furthermore the Mamluks regarded the Crusader enclaves as potential allies of the Mongols who remained the Mamluks' primary foes, while fear of an alliance between the Mongols and Western Europe dominated Mamluk strategic thinking. Unlike its Ayyubid predecessor, the Mamluk Sultanate faced war on two fronts, and the situation to their south, in the Christian Nubian kingdoms of what is now Sudan, was no longer as stable as it had been. Yet, as military rulers of a military state, it may seem surprising that the early Mamluk Sultans made few efforts to change the clearly delineated frontiers established in the mid-13th century. Apart from campaigns to remove the remaining Crusader-held enclaves, the only major area where the Mamluks attempted to control additional territory was in Nubia.

When seeking to understand the enthusiasm for Mamluk campaigns like that against Acre, it is important to realize that the Mamluk Sultans were not 'oriental despots' – whatever that may mean. They were simply the latest and most clearly defined of those 'warrior outsiders' who had dominated the Islamic Middle East for centuries. As such they governed

A seated ruler surrounded by his guards and civilian advisors in a 13th-century copy of the *Kalila wa Dimna* collection of stories, probably made in Egypt. The soldiers are clean-shaven Turks while the kneeling clerks are bearded Arabs, as in the early Mamluk court. (Topkapi Library, Ms. Haz. 363, f.6r, Istanbul, Turkey)

the main Arab cities, rural and semi-desert regions indirectly. Their actual power was also easy to exaggerate, as was the supposed helplessness of the civilian populations whom the Mamluks allegedly tyrannized. In reality the Mamluk government and army shared power with largely Arab civilian household or clan-based élites. At the top of the resulting power structure was the Sultan; however, he had few of the attributes of sacred kingship assumed by European rulers. Nor did a Muslim Sultan, unlike a Christian King, assume any privileged access to the Divine and instead had to negotiate with the existing religious establishment. For example, Sultan Khalil, the conqueror of Acre, once purchased a sandal that was reportedly worn by the Prophet Muhammad. Khalil wanted to wear it around his neck as a religious talisman, but he was barred from using such a relic for his own benefit. Instead Sultan Khalil had to establish the

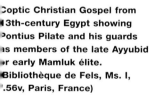

Coptic Christian Gospel from 13th-century Egypt showing Pontius Pilate and his guards as members of the late Ayyubid or early Mamluk élite. Bibliothèque de Fels, Ms. I, f.56v, Paris, France)

Dar al-Hadith al-Ashrafiyah or 'Ashrafi House of Religious Traditions', as a more suitable setting for the sacred object.

Another feature of this period was a revived spirit of *jihad*, not only amongst religious enthusiasts but also amongst ordinary people. This was directed by Sunni or 'orthodox' Muslims against Shi'a Muslims, the Crusaders and indigenous Christian communities which had made the ghastly mistake of collaborating with Mongol invaders against the Mongols themselves.

By the time of the Acre campaign, the Mongol Khanate of the Golden Horde in southern Russia and the Ukraine had nominally converted to Islam, which opened up remarkable geo-political possibilities for the Mamluks. What developed was a very practical if unofficial 'axis' including the Mamluk Sultanate, the Byzantine Empire, the Mongol Golden Horde and the Italian merchant republic of Genoa. The Mamluks gained reasonably secure access to their primary source of recruits, slaves captured by the Golden Horde. For the Golden Horde, the Mamluks were an ally in their bitter rivalry with the Mongol Il-Khanate of Iran and Iraq. The Byzantines found powerful friends and commercial partners at a time when the shrinking Byzantine Empire was under military pressure from several directions. The Genoese acquired allies, protectors and eager customers at a time when daring but discrete Genoese merchants ranged as far as China, the Islamic World and several parts of Africa.

And what of Africa, an area almost entirely neglected by European historians, but which played an important role in the leadup to the Acre campaign? For the Islamic Middle East, Nilotic and East Africa were more than merely a source of slaves and exotic trade goods. They were significant southern neighbours, linked by trade and religion. Though Islam was spreading rapidly, the still rather mysterious Christian kingdoms of what are now north-central Sudan, Ethiopia and Eritrea, were members of the same Monophysite church as the Copts in Egypt and the Syrian Jacobites of much of the Fertile Crescent.

Since the first wave of Arab-Islamic expansion in the 7th century, a system known as the *baqt* (from the Greek *pactos* or pact) had governed relations between Islamic Egypt and Christian Nubia while a tradition of mutual respect which went back to the Prophet Muhammad himself governed relations between the Islamic world and Christian Ethiopia. The Ethiopian church traditionally received its bishops from Egypt, but during the reign of the *Negus* or King Yikunno-'Amlak (1270–85) some senior churchmen had been recruited from Syria, undermining the stability of the Ethiopian state. Whether or not the Crusader states had a hand in this is unknown, but it coincided with a deterioration in relations between Ethiopia and the Mamluks.

Fears of an anti-Islamic alliance between the Crusaders and the Christian kingdoms of north-east Africa were not far-fetched, as the Portuguese would forge just that in the early 16th century. The Popes in Rome knew of these African Christian kingdoms, though their geography was confused, and by the mid-13th century there were ambitious plans to bring these distant peoples into the Catholic fold. Such moves could only have been seen in a threatening light in Mamluk Cairo.

The Mamluk Sultan Baybars had seized the Sudanese port of Suwakin back in 1266, probably to protect the Islamic pilgrimage routes across the

Red Sea at a time of increasing insecurity. The Mamluks hoped to continue good relations with the Nubian kingdoms – the northern kingdom of Makuria and the southern kingdom of Alwa, but Makuria seems to have felt increasingly vulnerable as more of the neighbouring tribes became Muslim. Amongst these were the Banu Kanz who have been described as 'Arabized Nubians' and who controlled the left bank of the Nile from the 1st to 3rd Cataracts.

Makuria consisted of the two ancient kingdoms of Makuria and Nobatia, with its capital at Dongola (now Old Dongola), a walled city with many churches, large houses, wide streets and a palace with domes of red brick constructed in AD1002 . In 1269 King Daud of Makuria sent a friendly embassy to Cairo but then, on 18 August 1272, a Nubian army sacked the Egyptian Red Sea outpost of Aydhab and that year raided the southern Egyptian frontier city of Aswan. Perhaps these raids were in response to Baybars' seizure of Suwakin, or because the Nubians wanted their own port, or because Makuria was having problems with the turbulent Banu Kanz who controlled the frontier region. Whatever the causes, the results were disastrous for Nubia. A Mamluk expedition in 1276 captured King Daud, replaced him with King Shekenda and inflicted massive damage on Nubia's fragile irrigation system. Shekenda was soon murdered but the next king was also soon deposed by Shemamun, perhaps one of the Nubian aristocrats whom the Mamluks had taken as political hostages to Cairo. King Shemamun in turn proved to be a cunning ruler whose reign formed a southern backdrop to the fall of Crusader Acre.

Events in Europe formed the western backdrop. Here the most significant event was the Sicilian Vespers revolt which led to a prolonged war in several parts of Europe between Aragon in Spain and the Angevin rulers of southern Italy who were supported by France and the Papacy. This massively changed the balance of power in the Mediterranean and was not stopped even by the deaths of both King Charles I of Naples and King Peter of Aragon in 1285. The expanding Aragonese empire was now divided between Peter's eldest son who became King Alfonso III of Aragon

A relief carving of the Lusignan coat-of-arms found at the seaward end of the wall around Montmusard. (Israel Antiquities Department)

and his younger son who became King James of Sicily. King Edward I of England mediated a partial truce in 1286 but thereafter Edward was himself preoccupied with his efforts to dominate Scotland following the death of King Alexander III.

Charles I of Naples was succeeded by his son Charles II who had the misfortune of being held captive by Aragon from 1284 until 1287. Though he inherited his father's claim to be King of Jerusalem, Charles II had to compete for it with the Lusignan rulers of Cyprus. Given Charles II's problems in Italy, it is not surprising that he put greater effort into maintaining Angevin claims in Greece and Albania. Here he had to compete with King Stefan VI Ouroch of Serbia who was extending his power in northern Macedonia, Bosnia and Albania, as well as with the Byzantine Emperor Andronicus II. These events also involved the culturally very mixed Byzantine Despotate of Epirus as well as the Crusader States established in Greece after the Fourth Crusade of 1204.

Given such volatile situations in the Middle East, Europe and Africa, it is hardly surprising that Acre's problems did not receive the attention that its inhabitants expected. Circumstances were equally unstable in the Crusader States themselves. King Hugh of Cyprus had been succeeded by his sickly son John in May 1285, but the youngster's authority was only recognized in Tyre and Beirut and he died after a reign of one year, to be succeeded by his even younger brother Henry II. Meanwhile the Mamluk Sultan Qalawun was preparing to attack the huge Hospitaller fortress of Marqab whose garrison had often allied with the Mongols, and which was

An Angevin army charging an Aragonese and Imperial force in a primitive Provençal wall-painting dating from the late 13th century. (*In situ* Tour Ferrande, Pernes-les-Fontaines, France; author's photograph)

not protected by the truce of 1283. After a month-long siege Marqab surrendered on 25 May 1285. Its loss came as a big shock and Acre, which had previously remained loyal to the Angevin claim to the throne of Jerusalem, realized that King Charles II of Naples was too preoccupied with problems at home to intervene in Palestine. Acting on the advice of the traditionally pro-Lusignan Hospitallers, the city recognized Henry II as king. Unfortunately Odo Poilechien, the Angevin *bailli* and commander of the French Regiment, remained loyal to Charles II and refused to hand over the citadel of Acre to King Henry when he arrived in June 1286. Only when the Grand Masters of all three main Military Orders supported Henry did Odo Poilechien relent – thus ending any real Angevin involvement in the Kingdom of Jerusalem, though the French Regiment remained. The fortnight of festivities which followed King Henry II's coronation in the Cathedral of Tyre were the last in Acre, and Poilechien was replaced as *bailli* by Henry's uncle, Philip d'Ibelin.

To further weaken the Crusader and Christian position, a fierce naval war now erupted between the two Italian merchant republics of Genoa and Pisa. In Acre the two rival communes fought on the streets, then, early in 1287, Genoa sent naval squadrons under Thomas Spinola and Orlando Ascheri to the eastern Mediterranean. Using friendly Tyre as a base, Ascheri attacked Pisan shipping while Spinola went to Alexandria to negotiate the Sultanate's friendly neutrality. Fearing Genoa's domination of the sea-lanes, the Venetians now sided with Pisa and although their ships were defeated by Ascheri outside Acre on 31 May 1287, they stopped the Genoese seizing the harbour. For several weeks Ascheri and Spinola blockaded Acre, until the city's civic leaders and the Grand Masters of the Military Orders persuaded them to return to Tyre. Meanwhile the lack of action by King Henry II of Cyprus and Acre showed how little power the nominal Kings of Jerusalem now had.

Further north the Crusader occupation of Lattakia was inconvenient for the merchants of northern Syria and politically humiliating for the Mamluk Sultan. Though now governed and garrisoned from Tripoli, Lattakia was theoretically all that remained of the Crusader Principality of Antioch, and as such was not legally covered by the Mamluks' truce with Tripoli. An earthquake then damaged its fortifications on 22 March 1287. Sultan Qalawun had already sent his *na'ib al-sultana*, Husam al-Din Turuntay, to crush the part-rebel part-autonomous Sunqur al-Ashgar whose power base was the castle of Sahyun in the mountains near Lattakia. Now the earthquake offered Sultan Qalawun an opportunity that was too good to miss, so he ordered Husam al-Din Turuntay to swoop on Lattakia with a rapidly assembled force. After a brief struggle, Lattakia surrendered on 20 April 1287.

Meanwhile Sultan Qalawun and his advisors had several other matters to consider, ranging from far reaching efforts to promote eastern trade – a commercial embassy from Sri Lanka (Ceylon) arriving in Cairo in April 1282 – to disrupting rival trade routes, which resulted in a Mamluk assault upon the Cilician Armenian port of Ayas in 1284. Closer to home there was also a low Nile in 1284, leading to a bad harvest and famine in Egypt. In January 1288 the Mamluks again intervened in Nubia, sending 'Izz al-Din Aydamur, the governor of Qus, to drive King Shemamun out of Dongola and replace him with his sister's son, Sharif Sa'd al-Din Sa'd. But Shemamun soon returned, expelling the small Mamluk garrison, the new ruler and any Nubian military leaders who had collaborated with the invaders. The latter included Jurays Sayf al-Dawla, the 'Lord of the Mountain' or commander of Nubia's northern defences. In Cairo, a month after the Mamluk expeditionary force set out for Nubia, the chief tax collector and chief religious judge of Damascus travelled to Egypt to complain about the Mamluk governor of Damascus, Sanjar al-Shuja'i. He was summoned to Cairo to be convicted of selling military material to the Crusaders.

One way or another, Sultan Qalawun had plenty on his plate. Most worrying were developments in the Mongol Il-Khanate of Iran and Iraq. Here the Il-Khan Abaga had been succeeded by his brother Tekedur who, though baptized a Nestorian Christian, converted to Islam and adopted the name Ahmad. This led to a revolt headed by Abaga's son Arghun with the approval of the Great Khan Kubilai in China, and Tekedur-Ahmad was assassinated in August 1284. The new Il-Khan, Arghun favoured Buddhism, while his chief minister was Jewish and his closest advisor was Christian. In 1285 Khan Arghun wrote to the Pope in Rome, urging common action against the Mamluks and, although he received no answer, Arghun persistently tried to form an anti-Islamic alliance with Western Europe. The series of embassies he sent to Europe are well documented but, fortunately for the Mamluks, never achieved the desired result.

CHRONOLOGY

1286

June 4: King Henry II lands in Acre but is refused entry into the Citadel.
August 15: Henry II of Cyprus is crowned King of Jerusalem in Acre.

1287

Early spring: Genoa sends naval squadrons under Admirals Thomas Spinola and Orlando Ascheri to the Eastern Mediterranean; Sunqur al-Ashgar, the rebel governor of north-western Syria, surrenders Sahyun castle to the Mamluk governor of Damascus.
March 22: Earthquake damages Crusader-held Lattakia; fighting between Genoese and Pisans continues in Acre.
April: Orlando Ascheri attacks Pisan ships off the Syrian coast then sails to Acre; Thomas Spinola sails to Alexandria to negotiate the Mamluk Sultanate's neutrality in Genoa's conflict with Pisa; a Mamluk army under Husam al-Din Turuntay marches against damaged Lattakia
April 20: Crusader garrison of Lattakia surrenders.
April 31: Orlando Ascheri defeats Pisan and Genoese ships outside Acre but is unable to enter the harbour.
June: Orlando Ascheri's squadron is joined by that of Thomas Spinola to blockade the coast of the Kingdom of Jerusalem; Grand Masters of the Hospitallers and the Templars join in persuading the Genoese squadrons to return to Tyre.
October 19: Count Bohemond VII of Tripoli dies childless; the mayor of Tripoli, Bartolomeo Embriaco, declares a republic under Genoese protection.
Winter 1287–88: Two 'merchants' go from Alexandria to Cairo to warn the Mamluk Sultan of the dangers of complete Genoese naval domination.

1288

February: Princess Lucia, sister of the late Count Bohemond VII of Tripoli, sails from southern Italy to Acre to claim the County of Tripoli.
March–April: Genoa orders Benito Zaccaria to send five galleys to support Genoese suzerainty over Tripoli; Princess Lucia arrives in Acre and the Hospitallers escort her to the frontier with Tripoli; the commune refuses to accept her and places their city under Genoese protection; opinion in Tripoli moves away from Bartolomeo Embriaco's republic in favour of Princess Lucia; Princess Lucia offers to confirm Genoa's existing commercial privileges in Tripoli.
September 4: The death of Sultan Qalawun's designated heir, al-Malik al-Salih Ali, results in Mamluk campaign against Tripoli being called off.

1289

January: Qalawun gathers an army outside Cairo; an officer in the Mamluk army informs the Grand Master of the Templars who warns Tripoli but is not believed.
March 9: The Mamluk army arrives outside Damascus then marches through the Buqai'a valley to Tripoli; reinforcements enter Tripoli.
April 26: The Mamluks storm Tripoli, subsequently taking Botrun and Nephin without resistance.
April 29: King Henry II arrives in Acre from Cyprus.

May 2: Peter Embriaco, the new lord of Gibelet, submits to the Sultan and is allowed to keep Gibelet.

July–August: Benito Zaccaria, having escaped from Tripoli, starts a naval campaign against Mamluk shipping and raids Tinnis in Egypt; King Henry II asks Sultan Qalawun for a renewal of the Ten Years Truce; Qalawun closes Alexandria to Genoese merchants; Genoa orders Zaccaria to end his campaign.

September: King Henry II sends a delegation headed by Jean de Grailly to impress the seriousness of the situation upon the Pope and other European rulers.

September 8: A Mamluk army leaves Cairo and heads for Nubia.

October–November: The Venetians decide to send reinforcements to Acre and Pope Nicholas IV preaches a Crusade in support.

Winter 1289–90: King Shemamun of Makuria retreats south and the Mamluks install a new king in Dongola.

1290

March: King Shemamun retakes Dongola and drives out the pro-Mamluk ruler, then himself accepts Mamluk suzerainty.

Spring: Northern Italian Crusaders sail in fleet of twenty Venetian ships to the eastern Mediterranean.

May 1290: Genoa concludes a new commercial treaty with the Mamluks; five galleys sent by King James of Sicily join the Venetian Crusader fleet on its way to Acre, reaching Acre in early summer.

July: Syrian merchants go to Acre to trade and Palestinian peasants bring food from Gallilee.

August: Crusaders attack Muslim merchants and peasants in Acre.

August 30: Survivors and relatives of this massacre take bloodstained clothing to the Sultan in Cairo, causing Qalawun to demand that the killers be handed over for trial, which is refused.

October: Qalawun orders a general mobilization of Mamluk forces; the Grand Master of the Templars sends a peace delegation to Cairo where Sultan Qalawun demands huge compensation for those killed in Acre; Rukn al-Din Toqsu is ordered to move to Caesarea and to prepare siege equipment.

Autumn: Reinforcements arrive in Acre from Western Europe and from Cyprus; King Henry II's brother Almaric takes command of the defences.

November 4: Sultan Qalawun assumes command of the Mamluk army outside Cairo.

November 10: Sultan Qalawun dies as the Egyptian Mamluk army sets out for Acre.

November 12: Khalil is proclaimed Sultan and orders allies and tributaries in Syria to prepare for a campaign next spring.

November 18: A suspected coup against Khalil is crushed in Cairo.

Winter 1290–91: Mangonels made of timber from the Lebanese mountains are constructed at Baalbek then transported in sections across the mountains to Damascus; Shams al-Din Ibn Sal'us is recalled from exile to be Sultan Khalil's vizir; a final embassy is sent from Acre to Cairo but the ambassadors are imprisoned.

1291

January–February: Troops are withdrawn from other Crusader-held enclaves to strengthen Acre; the Ayyubid army of Hama collects a giant mangonel from the castle of Hisn al-Akrad (Crac des Chevaliers).

March 6: The main Mamluk army under Sultan Khalil leaves Cairo for Acre.

March 25: The Mamluk governor of Damascus leads his forces towards Acre.

March 28: The army of Hama reaches Damascus where al-Muzaffar takes command of the Mamluk siege and supply-train.

April 5: Sultan Khalil establishes his HQ on Tal al-Fukhar on the eastern side of Acre and the Mamluk forces move into their siege positions.

April 6: The Mamluk siege of Acre officially begins.

April 11: Mamluk siege batteries start bombarding Acre.

April 13–14: Naval attack by Crusader ships against the right flank of the Mamluk line but the ships are dispersed by a storm.

April 15–16: A night sortie from Acre reaches the camp of the army of Hama, but returns to Acre after suffering many casualties.

April 18–19: A night sortie against the southern flank of the siege lines is unsuccessful because the Mamluks are not caught by surprise.

May 4: King Henry II arrives in Acre from Cyprus with his army and 40 ships.

May 7: Probably the day that King Henry II sends a peace delegation to meet Sultan Khalil, but they cannot reach an agreement.

May 8: Defenders of Acre abandon the barbican ahead of the King's Tower.

May 8–15: The English Tower, the Tower of the Countess of Blois, the walls of St Anthony's Gate and those next to the Tower of St Nicholas crumble as a result of mining and bombardment.

May 15: The outer wall of the King's Tower collapses.

May 15–16: Mamluk engineers erect a screen during the night, enabling Mamluk sappers to construct an access path between the inner and outer walls of Acre.

May 16: Mamluk troops advance under the cover of the screen and take the ruined King's Tower; Hospitallers and Templars defeat an assault upon St Anthony's Gate, which may have been a diversion; the Accursed Tower behind the lost King's Tower becomes Acre's key defensive position.

May 17: Mamluk units extend their control along part of the outer wall; Sultan Khalil orders his army to prepare for a general assault the following day.

May 18: The Mamluks attack before sunrise and by nightfall Acre is taken, except for four fortified buildings inside the city.

May 20: The Hospitallers and Teutonic Knights besieged in their headquarters ask the Sultan for an amnesty which is granted; the Templars similarly ask for amnesty but a fight begins and they close their gates again.

May 25–26: The Marshal of the Templars sends the Order's Treasury to Cyprus.

May 28: The Sultan offers the Templars the same terms as before but executes the delegation which emerges from the Templar headquarters; the defenders again close their gate but the Mamluks undermine the building and the landward side crumbles; a Mamluk force storms the breach and captures the complex.

July 14: Sidon falls to the Mamluks.

July 30: Haifa surrenders to the Mamluks.

July 31: Beirut surrenders to the Mamluks.

August 3: Tartus falls to the Mamluks.

August 14: Atlit is abandoned to the Mamluks.

1292

May: Sultan Khalil leads an army against the Armenian-held fortress of Qal'at al-Rum, which falls after a short siege.

1293

December 13: Sultan Khalil is assassinated by senior officers who fear that the Sultan's ambitions endanger the Mamluk state.

OPPOSING COMMANDERS

CHRISTIAN COMMANDERS

Henry II of Cyprus and Jerusalem was 14 years old when he was crowned King of Cyprus on 24 June 1285, but he did not immediately go to the mainland to claim the crown of Jerusalem because Acre was firmly in the hands of his Angevin rivals. Henry may have been an epileptic, and he was clearly unpredictable. He was reportedly also emotional, vindictive and occasionally cruel, never winning the real affection of his subjects in Cyprus or on the mainland. Henry II remained King of Cyprus and titular ruler of the lost Kingdom of Jerusalem until his death in 1324, apart from the years 1306 to 1310 during which his brother Amalric seized the throne – a long reign for a supposed invalid.

Amalric of Tyre was the eldest of Henry II's three younger brothers and was married to Isabella, a sister of King Hetoum II of Armenia. He was made governor of the Kingdom of Jerusalem in 1289 and remained so until the city fell. The Lordship of Tyre provided him with sufficient status to carry out his other duties, but Amalric did not get on well with his brother Henry II. Whether this resulted from the loss of Acre is unclear, but the King deprived Amalric's children of a claim to the throne so as to leave the crown to Hugh (the future King Hugh IV), the son of one of his younger brothers, Guy. In 1306 Amalric convinced the senior barons of Cyprus to depose Henry II on the grounds that he was incapable of ruling. Four years later there was a counter-coup during which Amalric was murdered.

Guillaume de Beaujeu became Grand Master of the Templars in 1273. He was at the time Templar *Preceptor* of southern Italy and Sicily where he forged links with King Charles I. Being distantly related by marriage to the king of France, Guillaume was referred to as *consanguineus* or cousin by King Charles and it was Charles who secured Guillaume de Beaujeu the appointment as Grand Master. Nevertheless Guillaume was already well known in the Crusader States, having taken part in King Louis IX's disastrous invasion of Egypt and three years later joining the Templars. He was captured during a raid led by Jean d'Ibelin, though he was soon ransomed, and became *Preceptor* in the County of Tripoli before moving to southern Italy. As Grand Master, Guillaume de Beaujeu adopted a conciliatory policy towards the Mamluks which annoyed some younger brother knights.

Jean de Villiers was elected as Grand Master of the Hospitallers in 1285. He had earlier been summoned to Syria in 1269, was recorded as Hospitaller *Prior* of Tripoli in 1277, and in 1282 was *Prior* of France, one of the most important positions in the Order. As Grand Master he travelled to Acre late in 1286 where he maintained the Order's traditionally close association with the Lusignan dynasty of Cyprus. In addition to his

complicated and often delicate political role, Jean de Villiers seems to have put great effort into making the Order of the Hospitallers as militarily efficient as possible and fascinating details of these efforts are reflected in surviving documents in the Hospitaller archive. Unlike the Templar Grand Master, Jean de Villiers survived the fall of Acre and remained Grand Master until his death in 1294.

Othon de Grandson was born around 1238, into the aristocracy of Savoy in what is now western Switzerland. Most of his career was in the service of King Edward I of England, where his post as Lord of the Channel Islands was probably to provide him with a regular annual income. Othon was, in fact, a man of Europe-wide importance who had accompanied Edward on Crusade before he became king, took part in some of Edward's Welsh campaigns and served in Gascony. Thereafter he was entrusted with assorted delicate and important diplomatic missions which included travelling to the Crusader States to prepare the way for King Edward's proposed Crusade. This never took place because Acre fell to the Mamluks, but Othon played a prominent role in its final defence. During most of the troubled reign of King Edward II, Othon lived in retirement on his ancestral estates overlooking Lake Neuchatel in Switzerland, dying there in 1328 at a remarkably old age for those days

Jean de Grailly remains a controversial figure, though the shadow that hangs over his participation in the defence of Acre probably results from the recriminations which followed the fall of that city. Like Othon de Grandson, Jean was a Savoyard and probably owed his initial advancement to the support he gave Queen Eleanor in 1265 when she used Gascony as a base from which to organize resistance to Simon de Montfort's revolt in England. Next year King Edward gave Jean de Grailly rich estates in the Dordogne valley and made him *seneschal* of Gascony. In 1272 he became *seneschal* of the Kingdom of Jerusalem where he also commanded the French Regiment. In 1277 he was back in Europe, serving as one of King Edward I's envoys to King Philip of France. Next year Jean de Grailly was reinstated as *seneschal* of Gascony but in 1287 he was found guilty of creaming off some of the King's profits. So he sailed back to the Middle East where he was made *seneschal* in Acre, again leading the French Regiment. He fought in the final defence of the city and, although badly wounded, escaped and spent the remainder of his life in his native Savoy, dying around 1301.

MUSLIM COMMANDERS

Sultan Qalawun al-Mansur al-Alfi was a Kipchaq Turk of the Burj Oghlu tribe, born around AD1222, who became a *mamluk* or slave-recruited soldier in his late twenties. This was much older than usual and consequently Qalawun never learned to speak Arabic fluently. His first master was a member of the Ayyubid Sultan's household and this man paid one thousand *dinars* for his new recruit – a very high sum which led to Qalawun's nickname of al-Alfi or 'the thousander'. He was one of the *khushdash,* or group of men freed by Sultan al-Salih. Qalawun subsequently became an important though not outstanding *amir* or senior officer when Baybars seized control of Egypt in 1260. Qalawun's own rise to power was, in fact, typical of the complicated and violent politics of the early Mamluk Sultanate. In 1279 Baybars' son and successor as Sultan, Berke, sent a Mamluk army commanded by Qalawun al-Alfi to invade Cilician Armenia, but when he returned to Damascus there was a quarrel between the young Sultan and his father's now senior *amirs.* Some older officers fled to Cairo which they tried to seize. Berke pursued them but was deserted by most of his supporters. Forced to abdicate, Berke was succeeded by his seven-year-old half-brother while real power now lay with Qalawun. By September 1279 Qalawun felt confident enough to proclaim that the state needed an adult and experienced ruler. Salamish was deposed and sent off to join the rest of his deposed family while Qalawun took the title of al-Mansur, or 'supported by God', as Sultan. The early years of his reign were very precarious, but Qalawun proved to be a highly effective ruler, and by the time he died in 1290 he was regarded as a truly great sultan, as determined as Baybars but more honourable to his enemies and more loyal to his friends.

Al-Malik al-Ashraf Khalil was Qalawun's second son, and became Mamluk Sultanate because his elder brother, al-Malik al-Salih 'Ali, died in 1288. His father had reservations about his suitability as his successor, once saying, 'I would never give the Muslims a ruler like Khalil.' There were even rumours that Khalil had poisoned his elder brother, though these were almost certainly false. Whatever his faults, there was no denying al-Ashraf Khalil's

The mausoleum mosque, hospital and *madrasah* school of Sultan Qalawun in Cairo, incorporating a Gothic portal from Acre. (Author's photograph)

Hama was ruled by an Ayyubid dynasty descended from the family of Saladin until 1332, long after the rest of Syria and Egypt fell under direct Mamluk control. (Author's photograph)

courage, nor his determination and, when politically expedient, his generosity. Khalil's main weakness was his pride and his inability to see that his position depended upon retaining the support of those powerful Mamluk *amirs* who had supported his father. In the end, however, it was Khalil's unrealistic ambitions which resulted in his assassination by a group of more experienced Mamluk officers led by Baydara al-Mansuri on 13 December 1293.

Al-Malik al-Muzaffar III was born in 1259 and succeeded his father as ruler of Hama and a considerable part of central Syria in 1284. The situation in Syria was complicated by Mongol invasions and the newly established Mamluk Sultanate of Egypt's desire to dominate all of Syria. By the time al-Muzaffar took control, Hama was under Mamluk suzerainty and the other local Ayyubid rulers had been swept aside by the Mongols, though a related Ayyubid dynasty endured in part of what is now south-

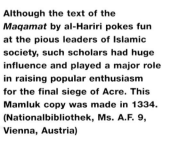

Although the text of the *Maqamat* by al-Hariri pokes fun at the pious leaders of Islamic society, such scholars had huge influence and played a major role in raising popular enthusiasm for the final siege of Acre. This Mamluk copy was made in 1334. (Nationalbibliothek, Ms. A.F. 9, Vienna, Austria)

eastern Turkey until the late 15th century. It has been said that the Ayyubids of Hama survived because of their obscurity. However, al-Malik al-Muzaffar III seems to have been a warlike though very loyal vassal of the Mamluk Sultan. Indeed the chronicler Ibn al-Suqa'i maintained that he had none of the qualities of his father who had been peaceful, whereas his son was violent and inspired fear even amongst his friends.

Ibn al-Suqa'i also provided a brief outline of the career of Husam al-Din Lajin who was a slave-recruited *mamluk* soldier of Greek or Prussian origin. As a senior Mamluk *amir*, Lajin had been governor of the Citadel of Damascus at the start of Qalawun's reign. When the *amir* Sunqur al-Ashgar, the governor of the city of Damascus, rebelled and tried to become sultan he imprisoned Lajin for fifty days. Sunqur's rebellion collapsed, Lajin was freed and became governor of the city rather than merely the Citadel. He remained in this post for eleven years, remaining loyal to Qalawun and marrying one of his daughters. As governor of Damascus, he was now the most powerful man in Syria and commanded the Syrian provincial forces at the start of the siege of Acre. However, Lajin was deeply mistrusted by the new Sultan Khalil and was arrested. After his release, Lajin was put in charge of the Sultan's arms as his *amir silah* but was again briefly arrested

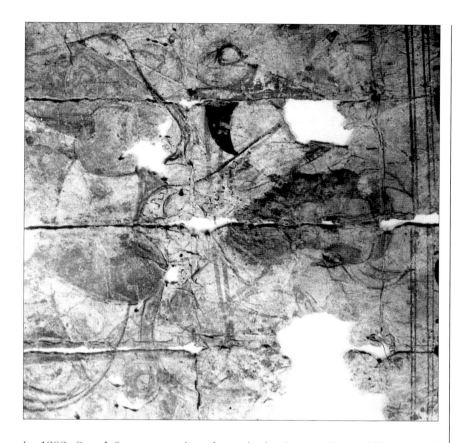

The Mamluks, like so many people in the medieval Islamic world, were often very superstitious. This good luck charm from Egypt shows the demon 'Jazrafil who rides upon an elephant'. (British Museum, London, England)

in 1292. Saved from execution through the intercession of Baydara al-Mansuri, Lajin was nevertheless publicly humiliated and when Sultan Khalil was assassinated in 1293 it was Lajin who struck the fatal blow, with the words; 'Let he who would rule Egypt and Syria strike a blow like this!' In fact Lajin did not become ruler of the Mamluk Sultanate until 1296, and was himself assassinated three years later.

Sanjar al-Shuja'i was another slave-recruited *mamluk*, probably of Turkish origin. He was made an *amir* of 100 at the start of Qalawun's reign, and became the sultan's *wazir* in 1283. Sanjar was literate in Arabic, suggesting that he became a *mamluk* at an early age and went through the full educational system available to élite recruits. By 1288 he was governor of Damascus where he earned a reputation for being competent, cultured and pious but also greedy. Sanjar became governor of Damascus for a second time in 1291. Before that, however, he commanded the Mamluk army which took the remaining Crusader enclaves after the fall of Acre. Sanjar al-Shuja'i married Baydara al-Mansuri's widowed mother, this being a normal way of forming family alliances. After the assassinations of Khalil and Baydara, Sanjar became *wazir* while his rival Kitbugha became *nai'b al-sultana* under the child sultan al-Nasir. They then competed for control but in 1294, after an abortive attempt on Kitbugha's life, there was fighting in the streets of Cairo which ended with al-Shuja'i's death. Kitbugha then purged his rivals, deposed the young al-Nasir and proclaimed himself sultan.

According to Ibn al-Suqa'i, Ibn al-Sal'us' full name was al-Sahib Shams al-Din Muhammad Ibn Uthman Ibn Abi al-Raja' al-Tanukhi. Born in

Nablus, he grew up in Damascus where his father was a merchant of 'middle rank'. As was typical for Arab men of his background, Ibn al-Sal'us travelled widely before returning to Damascus, establishing himself in business and earning an honourable reputation. During the reign of Sultan Qalawun he was a neighbour of the most senior civilian in the provincial government of Syria, and got a job in this man's office as an 'inspector and administrator'. Ibn al-Sal'us proved highly effective, especially as supervisor of the Damascus 'commercial police', and also became very rich. In 1290 he became inspector of his neighbour's office in Cairo, but soon got into political trouble, was arrested and exiled to Arabia. However, Ibn al-Sal'us was now a friend of the Sultan's son, Khalil, and when Qalawun died, Khalil summoned him back to Cairo to be the new Sultan's *wazir*. During the Acre campaign Ibn al-Sal'us was sent ahead of the army, first to Damascus and then to Acre. At the time he enjoyed the support of several very senior *amirs*, but the civilian Ibn al-Sal'us now grew arrogant. In 1292 he accompanied the Sultan against Qal'at al-Rum where his behaviour alienated several senior officers including al-Shuja'i. One of the *wazir*'s relatives wrote a poem to Ibn al-Sal'us, saying; 'Take care, O *wazir* of the land, and know that you have trodden on a viper. Seek God's protection, for I fear for you from al-Shuja'i's sting.' When Sultan Khalil was assassinated, Ibn al-Sal'us was accused of financial crimes by al-Shuja'i and died, probably as a result of torture, on 10 January 1294. Al-Shuja'i then summoned the author of the poem but, instead of punishing the terrified man, he said; 'You gave him good council, but he did not accept advice,' and rewarded the poet.

THE OPPOSING FORCES

CRUSADER FORCES

The army which defended Acre in 1291 had nothing in common with the first Crusaders which established the Crusader States at the end of the 11th century; nor even much in common with those who defended the same areas in the 12th and early 13th centuries. In military terms what remained of the Kingdom of Jerusalem was little more than an outpost of the Kingdom of Cyprus, largely dependent upon the Military Orders, Italian merchant communes, visiting Crusaders and mercenaries paid by European rulers. Tripoli was even more dependent upon the Military Orders while the Principality of Antioch now consisted of just the coastal town of Lattakia, currently administered from Tripoli. The Kingdom of Cyprus was itself a Crusader State and would long outlive the remnants of Crusader occupation on the mainland, but its military power was again very limited.

The supposedly 'soft oriental' habits adopted by the resident Crusader aristocratic élites was, of course, an acceptance of Middle Eastern customs which made sense, given the area's climate and cultural heritage. Military arrogance was more of a problem, and European Crusader forces had long spurned the advice of locals. Meanwhile the Crusader States benefited from the development of transport ships capable of taking horses and large numbers of troops directly from southern Europe to Palestine, as well as carrying substantial cargoes of food which the shrunken Crusader enclaves could no longer grow for themselves.

Meanwhile the Court and administration of the Kingdom of Jerusalem continued to take France as its model, as far as its limited resources allowed. The four major offices of state were the *seneschal, connetable, marechal, chambellan* and *chancelier*. The first was primarily concerned with ceremonial and justice, though its holder also inspected castles in the king's name, organized their supplies and changed their garrisons, though castle commanders answered only to the king. In war the *seneschal* fought alongside the ruler and it was the *connetable* who was second in command, or took over the military in the king's absence. The *marechal* assisted the *connetable*, organizing the army, paying mercenaries, checking equipment and discipline. The *chambellan* and *chancelier* were essentially civilian functionaries.

'The Crusaders besiege an Islamic city,' in a copy of the *Universal History of William of Tyre*, made in Acre late in the 13th century. (M.E. Saltykov-Shchredrin State Public Library, Ms. Fr. Fol.v.IV.5, St Petersburg, Russia)

Fragment of an early form of glazed ceramic from the ruins of Crusader Acre. The round shield and mace wielded by this warrior suggest that the local defenders adopted several styles from their Arab neighbours. (Israel Antiquities Department)

'The Martyrdom of St Just' on a late 13th-century southern French carved capital. The stiffened or semi-rigid protective collar was a typically Spanish or Catalan piece of armour. (*In situ* Church of St Just, Valcabrere, France; author's photograph).

In war the king had often been little more than first among equals and this was even more the case by 1291. His effectiveness as a leader depended upon his reputation for success and the strength of his personality. The military élite of the Crusader States had always been involved in war at an early age, less than fifteen years, and a man could apparently be called upon to serve until he was forty, but this élite had also dwindled into military irrelevance by the late 13th century. Non-knightly cavalry still existed but the strata of military status remained rigid to the very end, as shown in an agreement on compensation for deaths inflicted outside official warfare reached between Beirut and the Mamluk Sultan in 1269. It stipulated that a captive knight be released in compensation for a slain knight, a *turcopole* for a *turcopole*, foot-soldier for a foot-soldier, and a peasant for a peasant. In fact the 'Frankish' or European settler peasantry, never numerous, had by now disappeared into the cities or turned renegade so

Miniature effigy of Robert de Roos, made around 1285, illustrating typical knightly armour from England. (*In situ* Church of St Mary, Bottesford, England; author's photograph)

Effigy of Conrad Werner von Haltstatt who died in 1283. His advanced armour includes a coat-of-plates. (Unterlinden Museum, Colmar, France; author's photograph)

that the rural inhabitants of what remained of the late 13th-century Crusader States were almost entirely indigenous Arabic-speaking.

The Kingdom of Cyprus was organized, militarily and politically, along essentially the same lines as the other Crusader States, though there was a stronger Byzantine influence. The military strength of 13th century Crusader Cyprus is unknown but it seems that no more than 200 to 250 knights could be spared for operations on the mainland. Nor were such interventions particularly effective or wholehearted.

Mercenaries could be hired in Acre itself, often for service aboard ships, and now they were more important than ever. They included knights who held no fiefs but were paid salaries for as long as a ruler could afford them. Others were paid by lords and fief-holders to serve in place of perhaps no longer existing lesser vassals. Rich and powerful men also maintained mercenary forces, notably in the last anarchic years. In addition to the famous *turcopoles* who operated as light cavalry, other local troops also played a significant role in the 13th century, though the religious and social gulf between them and the dominant 'Frankish' élite remained wide. The Maronite Christians of Lebanon were, for example, effective light cavalry and infantry archers, especially in the mountains. Other parts of the coastal mountains remained outside the control of both the Crusaders and the Mamluks, their *jabaliyun* or hill-folk sometimes supporting one side, sometimes the other.

The Military Orders were dedicated to the defence of the Kingdom of Jerusalem, though this did not stop them from quarrelling with those who ruled or claimed to rule the Crusader States, and with each other. By the late 13th century these Templars, Hospitallers, Teutonic Knights and smaller Orders provided the largest and most effective standing armies in the Crusader East. They now saw themselves as the true guardians of the Holy Land, and resented outside interference. Of the smaller Orders, that of St Thomas at Acre was neither rich nor prominent, most of its money and recruits coming from England. The Order of St Lazarus accepted recruits from everywhere, all of them being lepers, though it should be noted that the medieval definition of

leprosy included a wide variety of incurable diseases. Attitudes towards leprosy were also more tolerant in the Crusader States than in western Europe, reflecting the less moralistic Islamic attitude which regarded leprosy as simply a disease rather than a sign of God's anger.

Another important source of late 13th-century troops were the militias. While the Crusader States lost great swathes of territory to Islamic reconquest in the late 12th and 13th centuries, the coastal cities expanded as refugees flooded in from the shrinking hinterland. However the urban commune of Acre was not officially recognized until 1232 while that of Tripoli was only recognized in 1287, shortly before the city fell to the Mamluks. Nevertheless, urban confraternities or brotherhoods had played a significant military role for years, forming individual units within the city militia. Most members were settlers of European origin, though the Confraternity of Saints George and Belian was for local Syrian Christians. In this way the merchants and artisans defended their walls and provided rulers with mounted or infantry sergeants. Yet, urban forces tended to be loyal to local leaders rather than the king, which could be a source of military weakness. The feudal structure had also changed as Crusader territory shrank, most of the land around a great city like Tyre now being held by the king or the Venetians while most of the aristocracy had money rather than landed fiefs.

By the late 13th century, major advances in the design of siege engines had profoundly influenced the design of fortifications. Stone-throwing machines were at least as important in defence as in attack, resulting in citadels and city walls having more numerous, higher and more protruding towers which served as artillery emplacements for the new trebuchets which could bombard the besiegers' more exposed siege machines. The outer defences of Acre were an example of this new system. By now it seems that Western European trebuchets were as advanced as those of the Mamluks, though fewer in number.

The triangular shield and large-pommelled sword carried by the knight on this fragment of glazed ceramic from the ruins of late 13th-century Crusader Acre were characteristic of Mediterranean Europe and the Byzantine Empire. (Israel Antiquities Department)

THE MAMLUK ARMY

European chroniclers consistently claimed that Mamluk armies were huge. In reality these forces, which outnumbered those of the Crusaders but not the more seriously threatening Mongols, were not particularly large. In fact the strictly *mamluk* or slave-recruited élite was small, which accounted for the Mamluk policy of concentrating most of their élite forces in Cairo. In Syria the indigenous population was more diverse, more dispersed, and was dominated by small Mamluk or vassal garrisons in the main cities. Of these vassals, the most important were the Ayyubid rulers of Hama and a substantial surrounding territory. They had close, though politically sensitive, relations with the Arab tribes living between Hama and the Syrian desert, the most important of which were the Fadl, Ali and Mira whose leader was sometimes called the Lord of Tadmur (Palmyra). Meanwhile the fall of the castle of Kahf to the Mamluks in 1273 removed the last independent Nizari (Ismaili or so-called Assassin) outpost in the coastal mountains.

The Arabic word *mamluk* meant a soldier recruited as a slave, then trained, educated and released as a full-time professional. Such troops, also called *ghulams*, had formed the élites of most Islamic armies since the late

Knightly donor figure on the late 13th-century *Icon of St Nicholas* from the Church of St Nicholas tis Steyis in Kalopetria, Cyprus. (Byzantine Museum of the Archbishop Makarios III Foundation, Nicosia, Cyprus)

An angel cuts off the hands of 'Josephus' in a 13th-century wall-painting in the village church of Ma'ad in Lebanon. (*In situ* church of Ma'ad, Lebanon; Dr. E. Cruikshank Dodd photograph)

RIGHT 'St Sergius and a female donor,' on an icon painted in the Crusader States in the 13th century. (Monastery of St Catherine, Sinai, Egypt)

9th century AD and the majority were of pagan Turkish origin. The Mamluk army which reconquered Acre in 1291 had its origins in the preceding Ayyubid period, in the armies of Saladin and his successors. The last real Ayyubid ruler of Egypt, al-Salih, had tried to reunify the fragmenting Ayyubid confederation by buying greater numbers of Turkish *mamluks* at a time when the Mongol invasions of southern Russia had uprooted the Kipchaq Turks, resulting in more slaves becoming available.

Al-Salih's élite regiments were taught to take pride in their *mamluk* background, and it was they who led the revolution which overthrew al-Salih's son, paving the way for the Mamluk Sultanate which emerged shortly afterwards. In this Sultanate *mamluks* of slave origin formed the foundation of both the army and the government. Nor did such *mamluk* 'men of the sword' feel any way inferior to those free-born civilian 'men of the pen' who administered the state.

The Mamluks' ranking system was highly structured. Beneath the Sultan himself was the *Na'ib al-Sultana*, viceroy. Then came the *Atabek al-'Asakir*, most senior military figure; the *Amir Majlis*, Lord of the Audience; the *Amir Silah*, Grand Master of Arms; the *Hajib al-Hujjub*, Grand Chamberlain; the *Ra's Nawbat al-Nuwab*, in charge of the ruler's

Bronze objects inlaid with silver and copper were amongst the finest products of Mamluk art in Egypt and Syria. Several include scenes of Mamluk military life. (Museum für Islamische Kunst, inv. I.3597, Berlin, Germany)

A famous Mamluk bronze basin known as the *Baptistère de St Louis* includes several battle or cavalry training scenes. (Musée du Louvre, inv. LP 16, Paris, France)

own *mamluks*; the *Wazir*, chief civilian official; the *Ustudar*, in charge of *mamluk* pay; the *Khazindar al-Kabir*, in charge of Sultan's treasury; the *Dawadar al-Kabir*, who selected which *Halqa* or non-*mamluk* troops would go on campaign; the *Amir Akhur*, in charge of the royal stables; the *Amir Jandar*, chief of military police; the *Naqib al-Mamalik*, in charge of military schools; the *Katib al-Mamalik al-Sultaniya*, in charge of registers of *mamluks*; and the *Malik al-'Umara*, a title given to senior provincial governors in Syria and Egypt. Within Damascus the most important military officials were the *Na'ib* or governor of the city; the *Na'ib* of the Citadel, the senior *Hajib* in charge of justice; the *Shadd al-Muhammat*, who looked after the Sultan's local interests; the *Khazindar*, in charge of the Citadel arsenals; and the *Naqib al-Jaysh*, commander of garrison troops. Outside Damascus there were also *Niyaba* governors of Aleppo, Gaza, and several other places, each with their own troops.

Senior Mamluk soldiers on the *Baptistère de St Louis*. The man in the foreground seems to wear stylised lamellar armour. (Musée du Louvre, inv. LP 16, Paris, France)

By the late 13th century the *mamluks* regarded Mongol military organization, tactics and even weaponry as a military ideal, while they believed there was almost nothing to learn from Europe. Although Mamluk armies relied on a combination of traditional Islamic and Turco-Mongol styles of warfare, they were more clearly structured than those of the preceding Ayyubids, and there were clear differences in status between *mamluk* and freeborn troops, with the latter steadily declining in prestige, most freeborn Kurdish troops were leaving Egypt for Syria where minor Ayyubid princes still reigned. Then there were Mongol refugees known as *Wafidiyah*, some 3,000 of whom arrived in Syria as fully trained warriors and were dispersed amongst existing *mamluk* regiments.

It is important to understand that medieval Islamic civilization had a different attitude towards slavery than that seen in western Europe. Slaves were much better treated and their status was quite honourable. Furthermore, the career opportunities open to a skilful *mamluk*, and the higher standards of living available in the Islamic Middle East, meant that there was often little resistance to being taken as a *mamluk* among the peoples of Central Asia and south-eastern Europe. Many young Kipchaq Turkish women, slaves and free, also arrived in the wake of *mamluk* recruits, bringing with them some of Central Asia's traditions of sexual equality.

Military science was taken very seriously, with practical text-books being based on the centuries old Arab-Islamic tradition of *furusiyah* 'military arts', which is why so much is known about the training of Mamluk forces. This was based upon the *maydan*, or training ground, at least one of which existed outside most cities. However, *furusiyah* was not a code of military conduct and loyalty like medieval European 'chivalry', but was a system of physical fitness and specific military skills which included lance play, polo, archery at both high, ground and distant targets, use of the javelin, sword fencing, use of a mace, wrestling, horse racing and various parade ground manoeuvres. Mamluk cavalry were trained to fight on foot as well as horseback, and to erect field fortifications.

Intelligence gathering was given priority, with political and military stratagems, elaborate ruses and the confusion of enemies being highly developed. Since the winning of political power in the Mamluk Sultanate was also egalitarian, in the sense that each slave recruit had a 'marshal's baton in his knapsack', the Sultan used similar methods to monitor the loyalty and competence of senior *amirs*. In strategic terms, the destination of raids and even major campaigns was kept secret for as long as possible, with commanding officers sometimes being given sealed orders to be opened at various points along the march. Consequently, even the best informed enemy had to disperse his defences. This also encouraged professional foes like the Crusading Military Order to develop their own spy networks within Mamluk ranks, though they never seem to have been as effective.

By the late 13th century, Mamluk armies were using remarkably sophisticated incendiary and even explosive weapons in siege warfare. The invasions which the Islamic Middle East had suffered from the late

11th century onwards had similarly stimulated notable advances in siege weapons, especially counterweight and other stone-throwing machines. In fact, Muslim artillerymen were so highly regarded that they were employed in Mongol China and Vietnam by 1282. By the late 13th century Mamluk mangonels included several versions, of which four were probably the most important: the *maghrabiyah,* or 'North African', a simple counterweight type; the *franjiyah,* or 'European', a larger counterweight version; and the *shaytaniyah,* or 'devilish', a lighter, rapidly erected machine, operated by men pulling ropes which could be swivelled to aim in any direction. The rather mysterious *qara bughawiyah,* or 'black bull-like', was called a *caraboha* in the Crusader States. It apparently shot large arrows and therefore cannot have been a true mangonel, and indeed the anonymous Templar of Tyre's account of the siege of Acre shows that the *caraboha* was a small, portable weapon which provided covering fire for men in the front line. As such it may have been an oversized crossbow mounted on a frame, or a variation of the torsion-powered *qaws ziyar.* The small number used by the Mamluks against Acre also suggests that it was expensive or highly complex. Some large mangonels had a range of 300 metres and could throw a 50, 100 or 225kg missile with great accuracy. To protect these weapons from counter-bombardment, they were normally used at maximum range.

The soldier fighting a lion on this early 14th century silver-inlaid bronze basin from Mamluk Egypt is equipped for combat on foot. (Victoria & Albert Museum, inv. 740–1898, London, England)

Mining was sometimes impractical against the Crusaders' low-lying coastal outposts because the mines filled with water. Nevertheless, the Mamluk Sultanate's highly organized *naqqabun* sappers, *hajjarun* masons, *najjarun* carpenters, and men skilled in the 'art of burning' were a force to be reckoned with. Wooden siege devices which had to be used closer to the enemy's defences, such as the *dabbaba* movable wooden shed and the *burj* movable wooden tower, had declined in importance because they were too vulnerable to incendiary weapons.

The question of when Mamluk armies adopted gunpowder remains controversial. *Siham khita'iyya* 'Chinese arrows' with *naft* cartridges attached were used in the 13th century, but it is unclear what *naft* now included. It originally consisted of distilled petroleum, but by the late 13th century it could sometimes include sulphur, saltpetre and perhaps even crude forms of gunpowder. Many of the clay containers found amongst the ruins of Crusader fortifications have very thick walls which could have added to any explosive effect, and it is worth noting that Hasan al-Rammah's *Book of Furusiyah and Ingenious War Devices* was written around 1280. He died in 1294/5 AD in his thirties, a respected soldier and living in

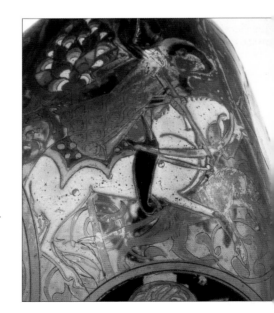

Damascus. So might Hasan al-Rammah have taken part in the siege of Acre? His recipe for refining potassium nitrate is not only very clear, but would produce an effective gunpowder, so it is hardly surprising that some scholars interpret some accounts of the fall of Acre as including references to gunpowder thrown by mangonels or attached to incendiary arrows.

NUBIAN FORCES

In the 7th century AD the Nubians, and particularly their infantry archers, were amongst the most effective foes that the early Arab-Islamic armies met. The result was a long-lasting *baqt*, or pact, which was a treaty between relative equals. While there is little to suggest that Nubian military capabilities declined over the next six centuries, there is similarly no evidence that they improved. As a result the warriors of the Nubian state of Makuria could not compete with the Mamluks who were now the most advanced and effective army in Africa. All the Nubians and their allies could do was retreat further up the Nile valley, carrying out a scorched earth policy as they went. They would then wait until most of the invaders had withdrawn, after which the Nubian army would return and blockade the tiny Mamluk garrisons which had remained in Dongola until it was obliged to return to Egypt. In fact, it was the unforgiving nature of the Nubian landscape which frustrated these Mamluk invasions. Eventually the Nubians had to accept they were the weaker party while the Mamluk Sultans had to be satisfied with imposing a tenuous suzerainty over their southern neighbour. Even so, the Mamluks' logistical achievements remain astonishing, operating as they were in an area which caused the mighty British Empire such difficulty at the end of the 19th century.

The little that is known about later medieval Nubian armies suggests that their archers still fought on foot, or perhaps sometimes on camel-back, and that their primary weapon remained a simple acacia wood bow similar to that used in ancient Egypt. Cavalry seem to have been more characteristic of the southern Nubian kingdom of Alwa, in what is now central Sudan, rather than Makuria. Few of these men had armour, and what mail they possessed probably came from Egypt. A remarkable iron chamfron, or headpiece from a horse armour found at the Alwa capital of Soba, almost certainly came from medieval Egypt.

The changes which had taken place in Nubia were political rather than military, with Makuria being feudalized during the 12th century. Despite a resulting reduction in the authority of kings and senior religious leaders, Nubia remained stable and prosperous. In addition to the fortified Makurian capital at Old Dongola, on a bluff overlooking the Nile, the last two centuries of Christian Nubia also saw much castle building, especially in the heartland of Makuria between the 3rd and 5th Cataracts. This resulted in massive brick and stone structures which largely remain unexcavated at Khannaj, Khandaq, Bakhit, al-Kab and al-Korro. Yet this was the northernmost province which provided Makuria with its most formidable protection. This had once been called Nobatia and it included a daunting stretch of Nile valley known as the *Batn al-Hajjar*, or Belly of

A Mamluk band with trumpets, two forms of drum and what might be shaken instruments. It was painted around 1315. (Freer Gallery of Art, Washington, USA)

Many Mongol warriors abandoned the Il-Khans of Iran and sought refuge in the Mamluk Sultanate where they were incorporated into the Mamluk army and almost certainly continued to use their existing Turco-Mongol military equipment. (Reza Abbasi Museum, Tehran, Iran; author's photograph)

ABOVE **The spear-armed horseman on this wood carving from Qasr Ibrim in northern Nubia probably represents a warrior saint, though he is represented as a typical Nubian cavalryman. (British Museum, inv. EA 71889, London, England)**

TOP, RIGHT **The Christian kingdoms of Nubia were a major link in the slave trade. An incised drawing on this fragment of 12th- to 14th-century Nubian pottery from Qasr Ibrim shows a spear-armed horseman with a prisoner or slave tied to his horse. (British Museum, inv. EA 71926, London, England)**

MIDDLE, RIGHT **The northern part of what was once the Christian kingdom of Makuria now lies beneath Lake Nasser, but further upriver the now Islamic land of Nubia remains much as it did in the 13th century. Here at Kosha the rocks of the Second Cataract are visible in the middle distance. (Author's photograph)**

BOTTOM, RIGHT **The long narrow strip of fertile Nubia is dotted with the massive fortresses which defended the Christian kingdoms for centuries. These tumbled towers and walls are at Debba. (Author's photograph)**

Stones, beyond which was the Egyptian frontier town of Aswan. In fact, the ancient rulers of Nobatia apparently evolved into the autonomous 'Lords of the Horses' who traditionally guarded this forbidding region from their own regional capital at Faras or Qasr Ibrim.

Dominating the desert east of the Nile was the Banu Kanz tribe, which claimed to have originated in Arabia before migrating to the Red Sea mountains of Egypt during the early Islamic period. There they intermarried with the existing Baja and Hadariba tribes to form a formidable force which occasionally dominated southern Egypt. In the 10th to early 12th century their leader, known as the Kanz al-Dawla, was sometimes recognized as the hereditary governor of Aswan, but the power of the Banu Kanz declined during the Ayyubid period and they were then fiercely persecuted by the Mamluks, being forced to withdraw into Nubia. Here the Kanz al-Dawla often provided the King of Makuria with his *eparch* or senior military officer. At other times they opposed the Nubian ruler, though usually the turbulent Banu Kanz proved a greater problem for the Mamluks.

THE OPPOSING PLANS

THE CHRISTIAN DEFENSIVE PLAN

The defensive plans of what remained of the Crusader States were based upon the assumption that they were economically so important to the Mamluk Sultanate that the latter would not actually try to destroy them. It was a pious hope rather than a strategic plan, but it was also based upon economic reality, added to which was the Sultanate's dependence upon the Italian merchant republics for trade links with Europe and with the Mamluks' primacy source of *mamluk* recruits north of the Black Sea. Despite their military weakness, the Crusader outposts had powerful fortifications, but royal authority had collapsed and the Patriach was in most respects the real 'ruler' of Acre. In this he was assisted by a council in which the *bailli* or royal viceroy was just one amongst a group of men with roughly equal influence.

When the final crisis came in 1291, Acre could only get enough troops to man its walls by withdrawing them from other outposts, leaving the latter with skeleton garrisons. Acre itself probably had a population of no more than 40,000 including around 1,000 knights and mounted sergeants, mostly from the Military Orders, and roughly 14,000 infantry, including mercenaries and pilgrims. The French Regiment still existed, though perhaps in reduced numbers, and consisted of well-equipped professional soldiers with experienced commanders. It was, however, designed for field operations rather than the defence of city walls. Another 700 troops subsequently arrived with King Henry II from Cyprus.

The Italian merchant communes provided substantial militias, stiffened by professional infantry. It also seems that the most skilled siege engineers operating Acre's counter-siege weapons were from the Italian communes whose fighting men probably took orders from their own *Consules* and *Vicecomites* in Acre. These were nominated by their home cities and were men with experience of the east. On the other hand, the primary duties of these Italian *Consules* and *Vicecomites* were to maintain order within their own commune rather than fighting in last ditch sieges.

Despite the seeming weakness of the defenders in the final siege, they had plenty of time to arrange their dispositions along the recently upgraded fortifications which included one or more barbicans ahead of the King's and perhaps other vulnerable towers. Quite what was meant by a barbican in this particular context is, however, not entirely clear. In Europe such structures were designed to keep the besiegers' stone-throwing machines and miners away from the main defences for as long as possible.

Acre's harbour was strongly defended by two towers. The Tower of Flies stood in the middle of the bay and commanded the south-eastern side of the entrance. It served as a lighthouse and had a small garrison

39

By the late 13th century, Italian military equipment was technologically ahead of the rest of Western Europe, as shown in this manuscript illustration from a late 13th- early 14th-century illustration of the 'Sack of Troy'. (*Historiae Romanorum*, Cod. 151, f. 9r, Staats- und Universitätsbibliothek, Hamburg, Germany)

to check the identity of ships before they entered harbour. A second tower at the end of the south-western quay was linked to the Tower of Flies by a floating boom. Storms were a major problem because the harbour was exposed to easterly winds which were common in spring and autumn, made worse by the collapse of the 9th-century eastern mole, which was now little more than a shallow reef.

THE MAMLUK OFFENSIVE PLAN

Mamluk strategy was remarkably consistent and, although the threat posed by the Mongols was far greater, the Crusader States remained potential allies of the Mongols who could provide bases for new Crusading expeditions from Europe. Ever since the reign of Sultan Baybars (AD1260–1277), Crusader-held territory had been steadily reduced and, whenever possible, the remaining enclaves were separated

Acre was one of the most
important commercial centres
in the eastern Mediterranean,
and the harbour was its reason
for existence. The remains
of the Tower of Flies still
stands at its entrance.
(Author's photograph)

from each other by campaigns to seize sections of coastline. Between such operations, the Mamluks made truces which were normally honoured by the Muslim side. On the other hand, the Mamluks took advantage of legal loopholes and political miscalculations by the Crusader States.

Mamluk siege warfare usually consisted of massive artillery bombardments to open a breach in the defences, followed by an assault if the garrison did not surrender. While bombardments were aimed at the walls and wallhead defences, miners usually excavated beneath the towers rather than the walls that linked them. The size and widely dispersed population centres of the Mamluk Sultanate was a strategic weakness, but this was largely overcome by superb communications services. Furthermore the Mamluks inherited the sophisticated administrative structures of earlier Islamic civilization. This made the raising, organization, payment and resupplying of Mamluk armies much more efficient than anything yet seen in Western Europe. It also meant they could move rapidly over long distances, along pre-prepared routes with supply dumps awaiting the troops at the end of each march. The Mamluks were said to number 200,000 at the siege of Acre, but this was a considerable exaggeration. The majority of soldiers were not élite *mamluks* and over half the people who took part were untrained and in many cases unmilitary volunteers.

THE CAMPAIGN

THE FALL OF TRIPOLI

A lead seal from 13th-century Crusader Tripoli, found in the ruins of Crusader Acre. (Israel Antiquities Department)

The final Mamluk campaign against the Crusader States began with an assault on Tripoli and again it was developments within Crusader territory that gave the Mamluk Sultan an opportunity to attack. Count Bohemond VII of Tripoli died childless in October 1287. His sister Lucia was married to Charles I of Naples' former Grand Admiral and lived in southern Italy, but Tripoli did not want a ruler so closely associated with the weakened Angevins. Instead, what remained of the County of Tripoli was offered to Princess Sibylla of Cilician Armenia. She wanted the Bishop of Tartus as her *bailli* but he was unacceptable to the leaders of Tripoli. An angry argument ensued, resulting in the ruling dynasty being overthrown and Tripoli becoming a self-governing commune headed by its mayor, Bartolomeo Embriaco, whose family had a feud with the old dynasty.

Bartolomeo also governed Jubayl, whose lord was still a child. Unfortunately he was of Genoese origin, which worried Venice and Pisa. A complicated situation became even murkier when a message was sent to Sultan Qalawun, seeking his approval for Bartolomeo Embriaco's takeover. Meanwhile Lucia arrived in Acre and was welcomed by the Hospitallers, allies of the Counts of Tripoli, who escorted her to the

The Citadel of Cairo dominates the city as did the later medieval city when the Citadel was the centre of Mamluk military and political power. (Author's photograph)

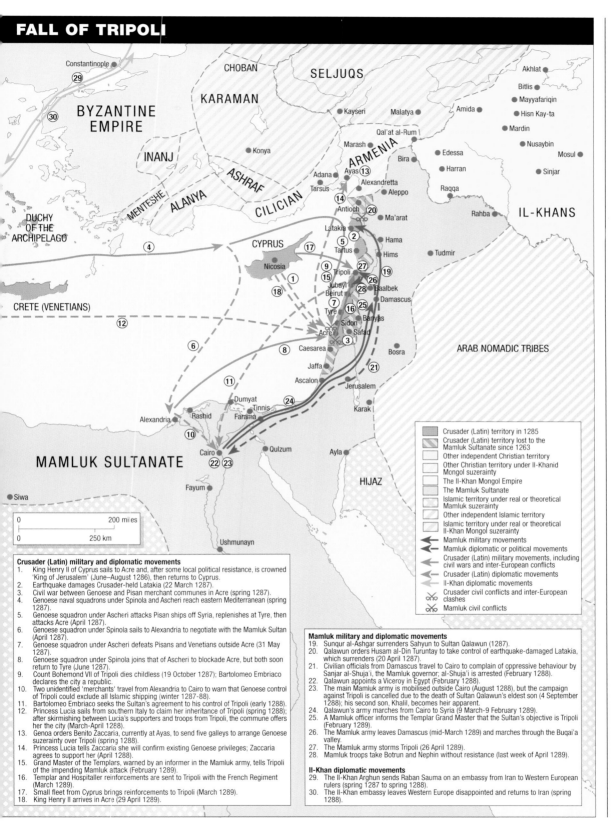

CHOBAN
SELJUQS
KARAMAN
Akhlat
Constantinople
(29)
Bitlis
Mayyafariqin
(30)
BYZANTINE
EMPIRE
Kayseri
Malatya
Amida
Hisn Kay-ta
Qal'at al-Rum
Mardin
INANJ
Marash
Edessa
Nusaybin
ASHRAF
Bira
Harran
Mosul
Konya
ARMENIA
Sinjar
Adana
Ayas (13)
Raqqa
MENTESHE
ALANYA
Tarsus
Alexandretta
IL-KHANS
CILICIAN
(14)
Aleppo
DUCHY
OF THE
ARCHIPELAGO
Antioch
(20)
Ma'arat
Rahba
Latakia
(2)
CYPRUS
(17)
(5)
Hama
Tartus
Hims
(4)
Nicosia
(9)
(27)
(19)
Tudmir
(1)
(15)
Tripoli
(26)
(18)
Jubayl
(28)
Baalbek
Beirut
Damascus
(7)
(16) (25)
Tyre
Banyas
CRETE (VENETIANS)
Sidon
(3)
(12)
Acre Safad
(6)
Caesarea
Bosra
(8)
ARAB NOMADIC TRIBES
Jaffa
(21)
Ascalon
Dumyat
Jerusalem
(11)
Tinnis
(24)
Karak
Alexandria Rashid Farama
MAMLUK SULTANATE
(10)
Cairo
Quizum
(22) (23)
Ayla
HIJAZ
Siwa
Fayum
Ushmunayn

	Crusader (Latin) territory in 1285
	Crusader (Latin) territory lost to the Mamluk Sultanate since 1263
	Other independent Christian territory
	Other Christian territory under Il-Khanid Mongol suzerainty
	The Il-Khan Mongol Empire
	The Mamluk Sultanate
	Islamic territory under real or theoretical Mamluk suzerainty
	Other independent Islamic territory
	Islamic territory under real or theoretical Il-Khan Mongol suzerainty
←	Mamluk military movements
←	Mamluk diplomatic or political movements
←	Crusader (Latin) military movements, including civil wars and inter-European conflicts
←	Crusader (Latin) diplomatic movements
←	Il-Khan diplomatic movements
✂	Crusader civil conflicts and inter-European clashes
✂	Mamluk civil conflicts

Scale:
0 — 200 miles
0 — 250 km

Crusader (Latin) military and diplomatic movements
1. King Henry II of Cyprus sails to Acre and, after some local political resistance, is crowned 'King of Jerusalem' (June–August 1286), then returns to Cyprus.
2. Earthquake damages Crusader-held Latakia (22 March 1287).
3. Civil war between Genoese and Pisan merchant communes in Acre (spring 1287).
4. Genoese naval squadrons under Spinola and Ascheri reach eastern Mediterranean (spring 1287).
5. Genoese squadron under Ascheri attacks Pisan ships off Syria, replenishes at Tyre, then attacks Acre (April 1287).
6. Genoese squadron under Spinola sails to Alexandria to negotiate with the Mamluk Sultan (April 1287).
7. Genoese squadron under Ascheri defeats Pisans and Venetians outside Acre (31 May 1287).
8. Genoese squadron under Spinola joins that of Ascheri to blockade Acre, but both soon return to Tyre (June 1287).
9. Count Bohemond VII of Tripoli dies childless (19 October 1287); Bartolomeo Embriaco declares the city a republic.
10. Two unidentified 'merchants' travel from Alexandria to Cairo to warn that Genoese control of Tripoli could exclude all Islamic shipping (winter 1287-88).
11. Bartolomeo Embriaco seeks the Sultan's agreement to his control of Tripoli (early 1288).
12. Princess Lucia sails from southern Italy to claim her inheritance of Tripoli (spring 1288); after skirmishing between Lucia's supporters and troops from Tripoli, the commune offers her the city (March-April 1288).
13. Genoa tells Princess Lucia to get Benito Zaccaria, currently at Ayas, to send five galleys to arrange Genoese suzerainty over Tripoli (spring 1288).
14. Princess Lucia tells Zaccaria she will confirm existing Genoese privileges; Zaccaria agrees to support her (April 1288).
15. Grand Master of the Templars, warned by an informer in the Mamluk army, tells Tripoli of the impending Mamluk attack (February 1289).
16. Templar and Hospitaller reinforcements are sent to Tripoli with the French Regiment (March 1289).
17. Small fleet from Cyprus brings reinforcements to Tripoli (March 1289).
18. King Henry II arrives in Acre (29 April 1289).

Mamluk military and diplomatic movements
19. Sunqur al-Ashgar surrenders Sahyun to Sultan Qalawun (1287).
20. Qalawun orders Husam al-Din Turuntay to take control of earthquake-damaged Latakia, which surrenders (20 April 1287).
21. Civilian officials from Damascus travel to Cairo to complain of oppressive behaviour by Sanjar al-Shuja'i, the Mamluk governor; al-Shuja'i is arrested (February 1288).
22. Qalawun appoints a Viceroy in Egypt (February 1288).
23. The main Mamluk army is mobilised outside Cairo (August 1288), but the campaign against Tripoli is cancelled due to the death of Sultan Qalawun's eldest son (4 September 1288); his second son, Khalil, becomes heir apparent.
24. Qalawun's army marches from Cairo to Syria (9 March-9 February 1289).
25. A Mamluk officer informs the Templar Grand Master that the Sultan's objective is Tripoli (February 1289).
26. The Mamluk army leaves Damascus (mid-March 1289) and marches through the Buqai'a valley.
27. The Mamluk army storms Tripoli (26 April 1289).
28. Mamluk troops take Botrun and Nephin without resistance (last week of April 1289).

Il-Khan diplomatic movements
29. The Il-Khan Arghun sends Raban Sauma on an embassy from Iran to Western European rulers (spring 1287 to spring 1288).
30. The Il-Khan embassy leaves Western Europe disappointed and returns to Iran (spring 1288).

The Templar Chapel in Tartus is still partially filled by poor modern houses. (Author's photograph)

frontier with Tripoli, but representatives of the commune refused to let Lucia enter. The commune had already sent a representative to Genoa offering to place Tripoli under Genoese protection. There the Doge sent a message to Benito Zaccaria, currently negotiating a commercial treaty with Cilician Armenia, telling him to take five galleys to Tripoli and negotiate terms.

By the time Zaccaria's ships reached Tripoli, circumstances had changed again. Fighting between Princess Lucia's party and Tripoli's representatives on the frontier resulted in the deaths of several people, perhaps contributing to a shift in popular opinion away from the commune towards Lucia who agreed to confirm Genoa's commercial privileges in exchange for Zaccaria's support. During the winter of 1287–89 two unidentified 'merchants' travelled to Cairo, warning Qalawun of the economic dangers posed by a Genoese domination of the eastern Mediterranean which left the Egyptian trade at their mercy. Qalawun took this as invitation to intervene and in August 1288 the

The site of medieval Tripoli is now the coastal suburb of al-Mina. Although it was almost abandoned, some medieval buildings survived to be re-used in later times. (Author's photograph)

The Great Mosque of Damascus was one of the most important religious buildings in the Islamic world. Here preachers encouraged thousands of ordinary civilians to help in the final campaign against Acre. (Author's photograph)

Mamluk army mobilized outside Cairo. However, the campaign was called off following the sudden death of Qalawun's eldest son and heir, Ali.

During his preparations for the attack on Tripoli, Qalawun prepared supply dumps along the army's proposed route. These may have remained, ready for a second attempt when the Mamluk army assembled outside Cairo in January 1289. The Templars' most important agent in Mamluk ranks, Badr al-Din Bektash al-Fakhri, now informed the Grand Master that Qalawun's target was Tripoli, but when the Grand Master Guillaume de Beaujeu warned Tripoli he was not believed. Instead the blow was expected to fall on Nephin, thus separating Tripoli from Acre. So Guillaume de Beaujeu sent Brother Reddecoer, one-time Templar commander in Tripoli, to repeat the warning.

Meanwhile the Mamluk army marched on 9 February 1289, leaving Qalawun's son Khalil in command of Cairo's Citadel, supported by the experienced *amir* Baydara al-Mansuri. The army moved via Salihiya, across Sinai and through Jordan to Damascus. The regional governors of Syria had also been ordered to mobilize in Damascus. A large number of infantry volunteers had also assembled, including many *Maqadisa* (Jerusalemites), descended from refugees expelled from Palestine by the First Crusade. A week after reaching Damascus on 9 March, the Mamluk army moved through the Buqai'a valley and appeared outside Tripoli late in the month.

Only when Qalawun moved through the Buqai'a was the threat taken seriously in Tripoli and all factions gave supreme authority to Princess Lucia. The Templars sent troops under their Marshal Geoffrey de Vendac, the Hospitallers under their Marshal Matthew de Clermont,

while the French Regiment arrived under Jean de Grailly. The crews from four Genoese and two Venetian galleys, plus smaller Pisan and other ships, were added to the defenders while King Henry sent his brother Amalaric with some knights and four galleys. Meanwhile many non-combatants fled to Cyprus.

No attempt was made to defend the great Castle of St Giles which stood some way from the city. Tripoli itself had the sea on three sides and a strong wall on the fourth. Unfortunately, some of its towers were old-fashioned and not in the best repair. Against these fortifications, according to the Templar of Tyre; 'The sultan prepared his siege engines, both great and small, and erected *buches* (wooden defensive structures) outside the town, and set up *carabohas* (*qarabugha* type mangonels), and attacked the countryside, and made mines underneath the ground, and penetrated the first ring of defences.' The Mamluk attack focused on the Bishop's Tower, the weakest part of the fortifications, and; 'The siege engines battered it so thoroughly that it was completely knocked apart. Likewise the Tower of the Hospitallers, which was new and sturdy, was split open so badly that a horse could pass through it.'

When the Venetians decided that it was impossible to hold the city, the Genoese admiral Benito Zaccaria also pulled back his own men. On the morning of 26 April the Mamluks launched a general assault against the damaged south-eastern wall and quickly broke in. However, the Mamluk army had suffered particularly heavy casualties and this was probably why Qalawun lost control of his troops, resulting in widespread massacre when Tripoli fell. The ordinary people suffered worst, while most of the Crusader leadership escaped by ship.

Tripoli was placed under control of Sayf al-Din Balban al-Tabakhi with a small garrison and within days the Mamluks also took Botrun and

After the fall of Tripoli, the Genoese retaliated for their loss of an important trading base by seizing a large Egyptian merchant ship off the south coast of Turkey, probably near the island castle of Korikos. (Author's photograph)

Nephin. On 2 May, Peter Embriaco, Lord of Jubayl following the death of Bartolomeo Embriaco in defence of Tripoli, rode into Qalawun's camp and offered his submission in return for retaining Jubayl under Mamluk suzerainty. All that now remained of the Crusader States was the narrow coastal strip of the Kingdom of Jerusalem.

DEALING WITH NUBIA

The conquest of Tripoli led to widespread enthusiasm within the Mamluk army for an assault on Acre, but Qalawun decided to deal with Nubia first. After returning to Egypt, an expeditionary force under the *amirs* 'Izz al-Din al-Afram and Turuntay was despatched southward on 8 September, accompanied by Prince Budamma, a claimant to the throne of Makuria. This time the invaders were welcomed by the Banu Kanz of largely Islamic northern Nubia, and the Banu Kanz leader Sayf al-Dawla Jurays helped the Mamluks to supply a larger number of troops further south than had previously been possible, though the Cataracts still obstructed their supporting fleet of Nile boats.

King Shemamun again retreated southward with much of the local population but a light column caught up with the fugitives fifteen days later, forcing most to return to Dongola. While Shemamun fled with his mounted retinue into the southern kingdom of Alwa, 'Izz al-Din came to terms with the *sawakira* or Nubian officers. They and the Nubian church leaders assembled in Dongola's Church of Usus (Jesus) where they proclaimed Budamma king. The Mamluk army returned to Egypt with hostages, including senior ladies of the Nubian royal family, and left a small garrison under Rukn al-Din Baybars al-'Izzi.

Five days later Shemamun reappeared, killed Budamma, purged the *sawakira* officer corps and allowed the Mamluk garrison to return to Upper Egypt. Makuria was, however, exhausted while the Mamluks were frustrated by their inability to settle the Nubian problem, so when King Shemamun agreed to recognize Egyptian overlordship, Qalawun agreed. After Qalawun died, Shemamun asked for the return of the King's mother because, according to Ibn 'Abd al-Zahir; 'kings, say the Nubians, cannot run their administration without women.'

In July 1289 Pope Nicholas IV had given the Fransiscan friar Jean de Monte Corvino an 'Explanation of the Faith' to be given to the Archbishop of Ethiopia in the hope of drawing Ethiopia into the Catholic orbit. Though Monte Corvino travelled to India instead, the Mamluk Sultan was concerned about this threat to Egypt's trade routes down the Red Sea. Within Ethiopia confusion had already been caused by a struggle for influence between the Coptic Church in Egypt, which was under close Mamluk control, and the Melkite Patriarchate in Syria, which had links with the Byzantine Empire and the King of Aragon. European merchants were already active in this area, and a member of the Vivaldi family reportedly reached the Somali port of Mogadishu from Western Africa in 1291. In September 1290 the Mamluk Sultan received a letter from the *Negus* or king of Ethiopia, announcing his intention of sending an embassy to Cairo with sacred candles and an Ethiopian tapestry, probably for the Church of the Holy Sepulchre in Jerusalem. The new *Negus* also proclaimed that, unlike his father, he protected Muslims within

his kingdom and wanted embassies to cement the traditional friendship between Egypt and Ethiopia.

After the fall of Tripoli to the Mamluks in 1289, the new lord of Jubayl hurried to the Sultan's camp to offer his allegiance in return for retaining his fief. (Author's photograph)

THE CRISIS FOR ACRE

The fall of Tripoli sent shock waves across the eastern Mediterranean and Europe. King Henry II sailed to Acre on 29 April 1289 where he found Sultan Qalawun's representative. Each accused the other of breaking the truce but Henry sent an embassy to Qalawun, currently in Damascus, asking for a ten-year renewal, to which the Sultan agreed. Around this time the Crusaders finally seem to have realized that the Mamluks intended to destroy them. Jean de Grailly was sent to Europe to ask for immediate help. Princess Margaret of Tyre had already negotiated another truce with the Sultan and in September Cilician Armenia agreed to hand over Maras and Behesna in exchange for peace, though it is unclear whether these opened their gates to Mamluk garrisons before the siege of Acre.

In April 1289, King Alfonso of Aragon had negotiated a treaty with the Sultan, specifically promising that Aragon would not help Acre if the latter broke the truce. The Angevin kingdom in southern Italy was embroiled in its own war with the Aragonese, which involved France and the Papacy in support of the Angevins. When Jean de Grailly arrived in Rome, Pope Nicholas IV gave him a warm welcome but as yet little else. England was meanwhile quarrelling with Scotland, although King Edward I did try to mediate peace between France and Aragon, resulting in the Peace of Tarascon in February 1291 – by which time it was too late to save Acre.

Central Europe was preoccupied with the future of the huge Kingdom of Hungary, where Venice had strong interests, and the southern Balkans and Greece were torn between numerous competing powers while Genoa, Venice and Pisa continued their bitter commercial rivalry in the Mediterranean. Unfortunately for the rump Kingdom of Jersualem, Genoa's interests did not necessarily coincide with the survival of Acre. Benito Zaccaria had escaped the fall of Tripoli and, in retaliation for the loss of a valuable Genoese base, attacked Mamluk shipping and raided the undefended Egyptian port of Tinnis. In response, Qalawun closed the far more important Egyptian port of Alexandria to Genoese merchants. Genoa ordered its wayward admiral to end his campaign and return both captives and loot to the Sultan. Genoa also negotiated a new commercial treaty with the Mamluks, adding another nail to Acre's coffin.

However, things were looking better for Jerusalem's representatives in Europe. In autumn 1289, Venice decided to send reinforcements to Acre. Pope Nicholas IV agreed to support them by preaching a Crusade. Edward I of England had already promised to go on Crusade, sending Othon de Grandson with forty to sixty cavalrymen to Rome in May 1289. Othon's main task was to arrange King Edward's Crusade, hopefully with the young King of Aragon as its leader. Unfortunately Aragon and the Papacy were at daggers drawn, though the Pope hoped that other European rulers would follow Edward's example. Meanwhile Othon de Grandson had met King James of Sicily and the young king agreed to lead 30 galleys and 10,000 infantry to Acre, but this was opposed by the Pope and Charles II of Naples. In the event only a handful of Spanish galleys and troops sailed east while James remained behind. After briefly returning to England, Othon de Grandson set sail for Palestine in the summer of 1290. He had very few soldiers with him, but expected to take command of the largely English Knights of the Order of St Thomas when he arrived, which he apparently did shortly before Acre's envoys to Qalawun returned with the Sultan's refusal to accept their excuses for a recent massacre of Muslims (see below).

The only significant response to the Pope's call for a Crusade was in central and northern Italy. Most were probably urban militias and mercenary infantry comparable to those who had long fought for the Papacy in its so-called Italian Crusades. The result was a fleet of twenty Venetian galleys commanded by Jacopo Tiepolo carrying a largely Italian Crusading army to Acre under the command of the refugee Bishop of Tripoli, assisted by Jean de Grailly and Roux de Sully from southern Italy. As this fleet sailed east in May 1290, it met five galleys sent by King James of Sicily who was officially still at war with both the Papacy and Venice. King Alfonso III of Aragon had also allowed the Master of the Templars in Calatonia, Berenguer de Santjust, to take forty horses, plus baggage animals, food, olive oil, other supplies and weapons to Acre, but it is not known whether these were aboard the ships sent by the Aragonese King of Sicily.

Meanwhile the Mamluk Sultanate and the Kingdom of Acre were watching each other carefully. Both sides employed spies and the anonymous Arabic-speaking 'Templar of Tyre' may even have served as a contact between the Templar Grand Master and his agent, the *Amir Silah* Badr al-Din Bektash al-Fakhri, who; 'cost the Master fine presents

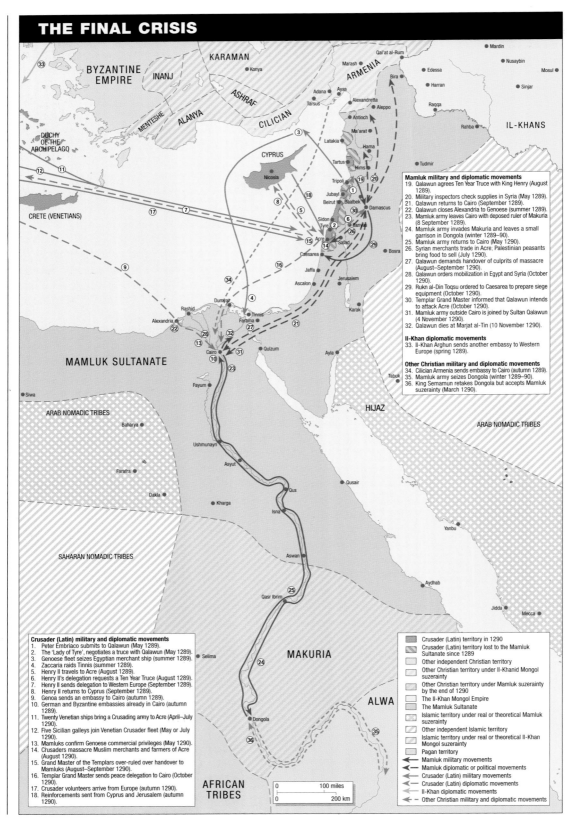

Mamluk military and diplomatic movements
19. Qalawun agrees Ten Year Truce with King Henry (August 1289).
20. Military inspectors check supplies in Syria (May 1289).
21. Qalawun returns to Cairo (September 1289).
22. Qalawun closes Alexandria to Genoese (summer 1289).
23. Mamluk army leaves Cairo with deposed ruler of Makuria (8 September 1289).
24. Mamluk army invades Makuria and leaves a small garrison in Dongola (winter 1289–90).
25. Mamluk army returns to Cairo (May 1290).
26. Syrian merchants trade in Acre; Palestinian peasants bring food to sell (July 1290).
27. Qalawun demands handover of culprits of massacre (August–September 1290).
28. Qalawun orders mobilization in Egypt and Syria (October 1290).
29. Rukn al-Din Toqsu ordered to Caesarea to prepare siege equipment (October 1290).
30. Templar Grand Master informed that Qalawun intends to attack Acre (October 1290).
31. Mamluk army outside Cairo is joined by Sultan Qalawun (4 November 1290).
32. Qalawun dies at Marjat al-Tin (10 November 1290).

Il-Khan diplomatic movements
33. Il-Khan Arghun sends another embassy to Western Europe (spring 1289).

Other Christian military and diplomatic movements
34. Cilician Armenia sends embassy to Cairo (autumn 1289).
35. Mamluk army seizes Dongola (winter 1289–90).
36. King Semamun retakes Dongola but accepts Mamluk suzerainty (March 1290).

Crusader (Latin) military and diplomatic movements
1. Peter Embriaco submits to Qalawun (May 1289).
2. The 'Lady of Tyre', negotiates a truce with Qalawun (May 1289).
3. Genoese fleet seizes Egyptian merchant ship (summer 1289).
4. Zaccaria raids Tinnis (summer 1289).
5. Henry II travels to Acre (August 1289).
6. Henry II's delegation requests a Ten Year Truce (August 1289).
7. Henry II sends delegation to Western Europe (September 1289).
8. Henry II returns to Cyprus (September 1289).
9. Genoa sends an embassy to Cairo (autumn 1289).
10. German and Byzantine embassies already in Cairo (autumn 1289).
11. Twenty Venetian ships bring a Crusading army to Acre (April–July 1290).
12. Five Sicilian galleys join Venetian Crusader fleet (May or July 1290).
13. Mamluks confirm Genoese commercial privileges (May 1290).
14. Crusaders massacre Muslim merchants and farmers of Acre (August 1290).
15. Grand Master of the Templars over-ruled over handover to Mamluks (August–September 1290).
16. Templar Grand Master sends peace delegation to Cairo (October 1290).
17. Crusader volunteers arrive from Europe (autumn 1290).
18. Reinforcements sent from Cyprus and Jerusalem (autumn 1290).

Crusader (Latin) territory in 1290
Crusader (Latin) territory lost to the Mamluk Sultanate since 1289
Other independent Christian territory
Other Christian territory under Il-Khanid Mongol suzerainty
Other Christian territory under Mamluk suzerainty by the end of 1290
The Il-Khan Mongol Empire
The Mamluk Sultanate
Islamic territory under real or theoretical Mamluk suzerainty
Other independent Islamic territory
Islamic territory under real or theoretical Il-Khan Mongol suzerainty
Pagan territory
Mamluk military movements
Mamluk diplomatic or political movements
Crusader (Latin) military movements
Crusader (Latin) diplomatic movements
Il-Khan diplomatic movements
Other Christian military and diplomatic movements

0   100 miles
0   200 km

Baalbek in Lebanon was a major Islamic frontier fortress throughout the Crusades. Its huge Roman temple complex became a massive citadel where ancient and medieval architecture stood side by side. (Author's photograph)

Winters can be bitter in Syria and Lebanon, especially in the Anti-Lebanon, yet the Mamluks and their allies hauled massive prefabricated mangonel stone-throwing siege machines through these mountains north of Damascus. (Author's photograph)

every year, which he sent to him.' Sultan Qalawun also had his agents inside Crusader territory, one of whom had been a *muhtasib* – usually an official who supervised the construction and loading of ships to maintain safety standards – called Jawan Khandaq whose name suggests that he was an indigenous Christian Arab. Whether he was the same agent reported inside Acre during the final siege is unclear.

The Crusader fleet reached Acre in early summer 1290 but the ships and their commanders, Tiepolo and De Sully, soon returned to Venice. Meanwhile there had been a bumper harvest in Palestine and, while merchants from Damascus came to Acre to trade, Arab peasants from Galilee also arrived with food to sell. Quite how the situation got so rapidly out of hand is unknown, but late in August some Crusaders suddenly attacked the Syrian merchants, Palestinian peasants and some local Christians whose beards made them look like Muslim 'infidels'. Some claimed it began at a drunken party attended by both Europeans and Muslims; others that a European husband found his wife making love to a Muslim, whereupon the enraged man killed several Muslims. What is clear is that many people were slaughtered, despite efforts by the Military Orders and local knights to protect them.

Some survivors and the relatives of those killed carried their blood-stained clothes to Cairo where they demanded that the Sultan take action. Qalawun demanded that the leaders of the riot be handed over for trial, but people in Acre would not allow this and instead tried to blame the victims for starting the trouble. Sultan Qalawun now got legal clearance from the religious authorities in Cairo to break his truce with Acre – a very significant move under Islamic law – and mobilized his armies. The Mamluks now established supply dumps along the army's proposed route, while the *amir* Rukn al-Din Taqsu al-Mansuri took his men to the area between 'Atlit and Caesarea to cut wood for field fortifications. These were taken back to Cairo while the *amirs* and Mamluk garrisons based in Janin drove the defenders of Acre back within their walls so they could not interfere with the coast road between Egypt and Damascus.

Although rumours were spread that Qalawun intended to campaign in Africa, Badr al-Din Bektash al-Fakhri informed the Templar Grand Master of the Sultan's true intentions but again Guillaume de Beaujeu's warnings were not believed. So de Beaujeu sent an unofficial peace delegation to Cairo where Qalawun demanded huge compensation for those killed or injured. The Council of Acre refused the offer and some members even accused the Templar Grand Master of being a traitor. A few reinforcements arrived, including forty brother knights and about 400 Crusaders with Burchard von Schwanden, the Grand Master of the Teutonic Knights, but he then resigned his office and returned to Europe. Hospitaller and Templar reinforcements also arrived, as did some knights from Cyprus. King Henry II's brother Amalaric took overall command while every able-bodied citizen was called up to defend the walls of Acre.

Sultan Qalawun had been unwell in October but decided to press ahead with the campaign. So, on 4 November, he assumed command of the army and the march began, but six days later he died. When this news reached Acre the people believed that the threat had passed. On 12 November al-Ashraf Khalil was proclaimed Sultan and almost immediately ordered the Mamluks' allies and tributaries in Syria to have their armies ready by March the following year. Governors and castle commanders were to assemble siege equipment, arms and armour, to summon sappers, masons, carpenters and soldiers while al-Malik al-Muzaffar III of Hama was to supervise the construction of new siege engines.

Khalil also sent a final warning to the Grand Master of the Templars, which was translated into French by the anonymous Templar of Tyre:

The Sultan of Sultans, King of Kings, Lord of Lords, al-Malik al-Ashraf, the Powerful, the Dreadful, the Scourge of Rebels, Hunter of Franks and Tartars and Armenians, Snatcher of Castles from the Hands of Miscreants, Lord of the Two Seas, Guardian of the Two Pilgrim Sites, Khalil al-Salihi. To the noble Master of the Temple, the true and wise, Greetings and our good will. Because you have been a true man, so we send you advance notice of our intentions, and give you to understand that we are coming into your regions to right the wrongs that have been done. Therefore we do not want the community of Acre to send us any letters or presents, for we will by no means receive them.

Acre did send a final embassy consisting of Philip Mainboeuf, an Arabic scholar, the Templar knight Bartholomew Pizan and a Hospitaller secretary named George, but true to his word, Khalil refused to see them. Instead the ambassadors were thrown into prison where they eventually died.

During the late autumn and winter of 1289–90, ships full of refugees sailed from Acre to Cyprus. Some men of fighting age also left, along with some of the richer merchants. Within the city the Pisans built a particularly large stone-throwing mangonel and in January and February 1291 many troops were withdrawn from other Crusader enclaves to strengthen Acre.

A suspected plot to overthrow Sultan Khalil was crushed in Cairo and on 18 November Husam al-Din Turantay was arrested, along with several other senior *amirs*. Turantay was soon released but died within a few days. Sunqur al-Massah, the *amir* in command of Mamluk forces outside Acre, was accused of conspiring with the enemy, probably having been implicated in Turantay's supposed plot, and Shams al-Din Sal'us was recalled from exile in the Hijaz to be the new Sultan's *wazir*.

The Mamluk government now focused on raising enthusiasm for the forthcoming campaign and Islam now played as great a part as Christianity had for the First Crusade. It was apparent in all ranks of society, and the Mamluk *amir* of Karak, Baybars al-Mansuri, later described his enthusiasm; 'My soul had a strong desire for *jihad*, a desire for it like the earth thirsts for delivering rain.' A week before the main army set out, religious and other notables assembled in Qalawun's mausoleum in Cairo for a complete recitation of the Koran while the Sultan distributed money to the poor and those who lived in religious convents. News of the forthcoming campaign had been accompanied by a call for *ghuzat* volunteers in the mosques, such men eventually outnumbering the regular soldiers, and the entire population of Damascus would help move the huge new mangonels that had been constructed in the city.

The manufacture of new mangonels continued throughout the winter, approximately 100 being made in Cairo and Damascus. Most would have been small anti-personnel weapons, but the *amir* Shams al-Din al-A'sar al-Mushidd was sent to fell the notably tall trees of the Lebanon's Wadi al-Murabbin. They were taken to Baalbek and made into the largest mangonels yet seen which, disassembled, were then transported to Damascus, despite huge problems with the weather. Snow similarly hampered the army of Hama as it transported a large mangonel nicknamed the *Mansuri*. The historian Abu'l-Fida was a junior 'amir of ten' at the time and was in charge of one waggon. 'Rain and snow struck us between Hisn al-Akrad and Damascus, causing great hardship, for the waggons were heavy and the oxen weak and dying of cold.' Consequently it took Abu'l-Fida and his colleagues a month to march from Hisn al-Akrad to Acre, usually an eight-day ride. The Mamluks eventually arrayed more mangonels against Acre than they had ever used before: 72 such weapons, according to the most reliable sources. Al-Yunini stated that 15 were of the largest *ifranji* type, while al-'Ayni stated that 52 were of the smaller though still powerful man-powered traction *shaytaniyah* type.

DISPOSITION OF MAMLUK FORCES AROUND ACRE AT THE START OF THE SIEGE (5 April to 14 April 1291)

(Note: The medieval sea level was 2 metres lower than today)

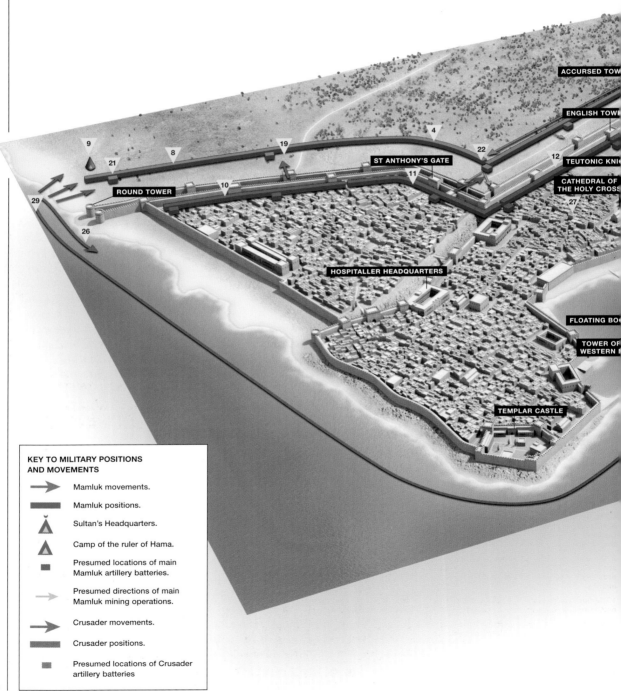

ACCURSED TOW

ENGLISH TOW

4

9

19

21

8

ST ANTHONY'S GATE

22

12

TEUTONIC KNI

ROUND TOWER

10

11

CATHEDRAL OF THE HOLY CROSS

29

27

26

HOSPITALLER HEADQUARTERS

FLOATING BO

TOWER OF WESTERN

TEMPLAR CASTLE

KEY TO MILITARY POSITIONS AND MOVEMENTS

Mamluk movements.

Mamluk positions.

Sultan's Headquarters.

Camp of the ruler of Hama.

Presumed locations of main Mamluk artillery batteries.

Presumed directions of main Mamluk mining operations.

Crusader movements.

Crusader positions.

Presumed locations of Crusader artillery batteries

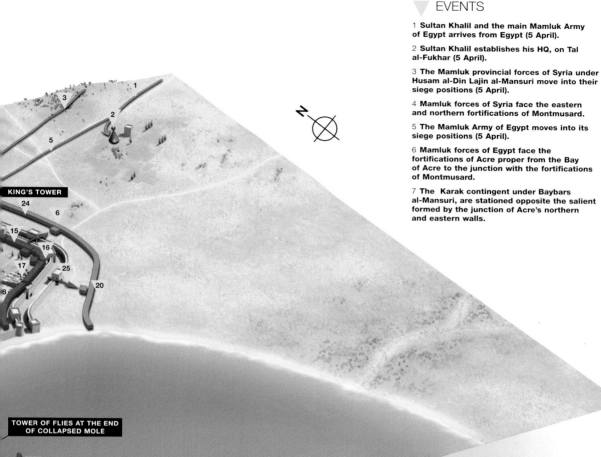

KING'S TOWER

24

6

15

16

17   25

20

8

1

3

2

5

TOWER OF FLIES AT THE END
OF COLLAPSED MOLE

28

▼ EVENTS

1 **Sultan Khalil and the main Mamluk Army of Egypt arrives from Egypt (5 April).**

2 **Sultan Khalil establishes his HQ, on Tal al-Fukhar (5 April).**

3 **The Mamluk provincial forces of Syria under Husam al-Din Lajin al-Mansuri move into their siege positions (5 April).**

4 **Mamluk forces of Syria face the eastern and northern fortifications of Montmusard.**

5 **The Mamluk Army of Egypt moves into its siege positions (5 April).**

6 **Mamluk forces of Egypt face the fortifications of Acre proper from the Bay of Acre to the junction with the fortifications of Montmusard.**

7 **The Karak contingent under Baybars al-Mansuri, are stationed opposite the salient formed by the junction of Acre's northern and eastern walls.**

8 **The army of the Ayyubid vassal-ruler of Hama, al-Malik al-Muzaffar, takes its traditional position on the right flank of the Mamluk army (5 April).**

9 **The camp of al-Muzaffar and his army is some distance to the rear of the siege lines, probably between the beach and the coastal marsh.**

10 **Templars man walls and towers along the northern fortifications of Montmusard.**

11 **Hospitallers man walls and towers along the eastern fortifications of Montmusard, and perhaps also part of the northern wall of Acre proper.**

12 **Teutonic knights are believed to have manned the walls and towers next to the forces of King Henry II, probably to their left.**

13A-B **Troops of the ruler of Cyprus and the Kingdom of Jerusalem commanded by King Henry II's brother Amalric, are stationed at the most vulnerable part of the fortifications, at the angle of the King's Tower and probably the barbican ahead of it.**

14 **French Crusaders under Jean de Grailly.**

15 **English Crusaders under Othon de Grandson.**

16 **Venetian troops or communal militia; perhaps also including the Northern Italian Crusaders who arrived in 1290 AD.**

17 **Pisan troops or communal militia.**

18 **The urban militia of Acre.**

19 **At first the defenders did not close the gates of Acre, and they occasionally emerged to 'skirmish' with the enemy, probably attempting to hinder the construction of Mamluk siege batteries (5 to 10 or 11 April).**

20 **A giant mangonel called 'The Victorious' facing the Pisans.**

21 **A giant mangonel called 'The Furious' facing the Templars.**

22 **Another giant mangonel facing the Hospitallers.**

23 **A machine on wheels was erected facing the salient formed by the Accursed Tower; this is likely to have been a protective shield for miners and sappers.**

24 **Numbers of large mangonel balls have been found in what had been the Cemetery of St Nicholas; perhaps from a Mamluk munitions store.**

25 **Large and small mangonel balls and a ceramic 'fire-bomb' were found in this area; some probably shot by the mangonel called 'The Victorious'.**

26 **Large mangonel balls were found in this area; probably shot by the mangonel called 'The Furious'.**

27 **Several mangonel balls ranging from 40 to 75 kgs weight were found in this area which may have served as a munitions store.**

28 **Large merchant ships had to moor outside the harbour, cargoes and passengers being ferried to the wharves by smaller craft.**

29 **Naval attack by several Crusader ships against the army of Hama on the right flank of the Mamluk line; one Crusader ship was mounted with a mangonel while other smaller craft carried crossbowmen or landed troops to harass the Hama camp (probably on 13 or 14 April); these were dispersed by a storm.**

About five *qara bughawiyah* 'black-bull' anti-personnel machines were also used. These shot javelin-like arrows and one name suggests a giant crossbow or tension-powered weapon. Numerous *lu'bah* mangonels were ranged against the city, but these were not included in the overall figures as they were small anti-personnel machines.

THE SIEGE OF ACRE

'Izz al-Din al-Afram, who had previously fought in Nubia, arrived in Damascus on 3 March 1291 to supervise the transport of siege equipment to Acre. It took several days to get everything on the road and the last detachment, commanded by Husam al-Din Lajin, only left Damascus on 23 March. That same day al-Malik al-Muzaffar of Hama arrived, followed by his army and siege equipment on the 26th. Next day other forces from central Syria reached Damascus, led by Sayf al-Din Balban al-Tabakhi. However, no troops came from northern Syria, presumably because they had to defend the frontier with the ever-threatening Mongols.

On 6 March Sultan Khalil and the main army of Egypt set off from Cairo, across Sinai to Gaza where they were joined by Baybars al-Mansuri with the troops of Karak before continuing to Acre.

The assembling of Mamluk forces from different locations, considerable distances and across very difficult terrain, reaching their destinations in a coordinated sequence without confusion or shortage of supplies was a remarkable tribute to Mamluk military organization. Meanwhile an advance guard appeared outside Acre early in March, forcing European settlers to abandon the outlying villages and leading to more women, children and old men being sent to safety in Cyprus.

Sultan Khalil reached Acre on 5 April and established his headquarters on Tal al-Fukhar just east of the city, whereupon the entire Mamluk army moved forward into its siege positions with the Ayyubid army of Hama adopting its traditional position on the extreme right wing. The Templar of Tyre witnessed events: 'The sultan pitched his tents very close together,

The north-eastern corner of the existing inner wall of the Old City of Acre. The lower part of the wall on the right may be partially Crusader. (Author's photograph)

The inner northern wall of Acre, seen across the intervening moat from the outer wall, with the 18th-century Ahmad al-Jazzar Mosque in the distance. The inner wall follows the line of the medieval fortifications, though the outer wall was added many centuries later. (Author's photograph)

A 13th-century ceramic camel with a small howdah on its back. Large numbers of camels were used as baggage animals by the Mamluk army. (Museum of Islamic Art, inv. 14358, Cairo, Egypt; author's photograph)

from Toron all the way up to al-Sumairiya, so that the whole plain was covered with tents. The tent of the sultan himself, which is called the *dahlis* (Arabic for vestibule or reception room) was on a small hill, where there was a lovely tower and gardens and vineyards of the Templars. This *dahlis* was entirely red, and its door opened facing the city of Acre.' The siege of Acre formally began next day; meanwhile part of the Sultan's harem arrived in Damascus on 9 April.

There followed just over a week of skirmishing, as was normal in the initial stages of a siege, and the Crusaders did not yet close their main gates. Whether the defenders suffered so many casualties that they retreated inside their walls, or closed their gates once the enemy siege lines came too close, is unclear. According to one eyewitness, the *amir* Sayf al-Din Ibn al-Mihaffadar, it took the Muslims two days to erect their mangonels and most sources agree that the bombardment began on 11 April. According to the Templar of Tyre, 'One of these (Mamluk) engines was called *Ghadban*, that is to say Furious, and it was set up in front of the Templars' section. Another which shot at the Pisans' section was called *al-Mansuri*, that is to say Victory. Yet another, very large, whose name I do not know, shot at the Hospitallers' section, and a fourth engine shot at the great tower called the Accursed Tower.' Islamic sources state that the stones shot by the largest of the defenders' fifteen mangonels weighed 45 kgs.

The Mamluk siege-lines consisted of defensive positions, ditches, palisades and portable wooden shelters. Acre was now bombarded daily with rocks, incendiaries and crude explosives as the Mamluk army inched forwards. The Templar of Tyre's detailed and personal account cannot be bettered: 'They set up great barricades and wicker screens,

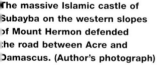

The massive Islamic castle of Subayba on the western slopes of Mount Hermon defended the road between Acre and Damascus. (Author's photograph)

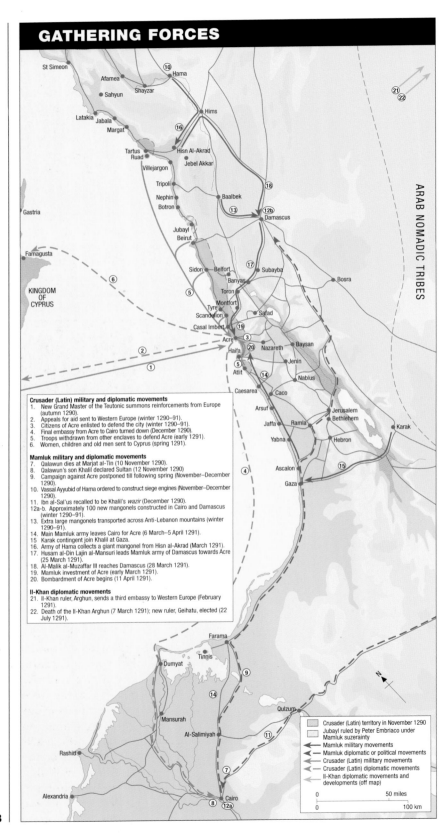

Crusader (Latin) military and diplomatic movements
1. New Grand Master of the Teutonic summons reinforcements from Europe (autumn 1290).
2. Appeals for aid sent to Western Europe (winter 1290–91).
3. Citizens of Acre enlisted to defend the city (winter 1290–91).
4. Final embassy from Acre to Cairo turned down (December 1290).
5. Troops withdrawn from other enclaves to defend Acre (early 1291).
6. Women, children and old men sent to Cyprus (spring 1291).

Mamluk military and diplomatic movements
7. Qalawun dies at Marjat al-Tin (10 November 1290).
8. Qalawun's son Khalil declared Sultan (12 November 1290)
9. Campaign against Acre postponed till following spring (November–December 1290).
10. Vassal Ayyubid of Hama ordered to construct siege engines (November–December 1290).
11. Ibn al-Sal'us recalled to be Khalil's *wazir* (December 1290).
12a-b. Approximately 100 new mangonels constructed in Cairo and Damascus (winter 1290–91).
13. Extra large mangonels transported across Anti-Lebanon mountains (winter 1290–91).
14. Main Mamluk army leaves Cairo for Acre (6 March–5 April 1291).
15. Karak contingent join Khalil at Gaza.
16. Army of Hama collects a giant mangonel from Hisn al-Akrad (March 1291).
17. Husam al-Din Lajin al-Mansuri leads Mamluk army of Damascus towards Acre (25 March 1291).
18. Al-Malik al-Muzaffar III reaches Damascus (28 March 1291).
19. Mamluk investment of Acre (early March 1291).
20. Bombardment of Acre begins (11 April 1291).

Il-Khan diplomatic movements
21. Il-Khan ruler, Arghun, sends a third embassy to Western Europe (February 1291).
22. Death of the Il-Khan Arghun (7 March 1291); new ruler, Geihatu, elected (22 July 1291).

ARAB NOMADIC TRIBES

KINGDOM OF CYPRUS

	Crusader (Latin) territory in November 1290
	Jubayl ruled by Peter Embriaco under Mamluk suzerainty
←	Mamluk military movements
◄	Mamluk diplomatic or political movements
←	Crusader (Latin) military movements
◄	Crusader (Latin) diplomatic movements
→	Il-Khan diplomatic movements and developments (off map)

0   50 miles
0   100 km

Looking westwards from the Burj al-Commandar, along the line of what would have been the northern wall of the eastern part of Crusader Acre. Beyond the prominent cypress tree right of centre is the low Tal al-Fukhar where Sultan Khalil had his headquarters. (Author's photograph)

Although the Crusaders still controlled Mount Carmel and the castle of Atlit in 1291, they were separated by the narrow strip of Mamluk-held coast in the centre of this picture. (Author's photograph)

ringing the walls with them the first night, and the second night they moved them further in, and on the third night further still. And they brought them so far forward that they came up to the lip of the moat. Behind these screens the armed men dismounted from their horses, bows in hand.' The defenders could not stop this advance because 'These people had their horsemen fully armed, on armoured horses, and they stretched from one side of the city to the other... There were more than 15,000 of them (an exaggeration), and they worked in four shifts a day, so that no one was overworked.' Furthermore, the men on armoured horses each carried five bundles of brushwood on the necks of their horses; 'And when night came they put them in front of the screens, and bound a cord on top, and the pile became like a wall that no engine could harm, though some of our medium engines shot and battered at it without effect. The stones merely rebounded into the moat.... After this the enemy brought up their *carabohas*, small hand-

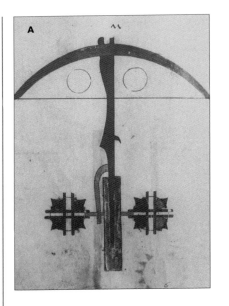

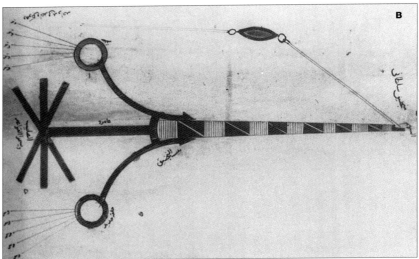

The most detailed surviving text concerning siege machines is the late medieval *Kitab al-'Aniq fi'l-Manajaniq* by Ibn Urunbugha al-Zardkash, though the weapons he describes are the same as those used in the late 13th century. A: *qaws al-'aqqar* large form of crossbow spanned by a winch. B: *manjaniq sultani* beamsling mangonel operated by teams pulling ropes. C: raising the *sahm* beamsling onto the largest form of counterweight trebuchet. (Topkapi Library, Ms. Ahmad III, 3469, Istanbul, Turkey)

operated Turkish devices with a high rate of shooting which did more damage to our men than the larger engines did, since in the places where the *carabohas* were shooting, no one dared to come out into the open.' Several fortifications were undermined, including the Tower of the Countess of Blois, the barbican ahead of the Accursed Tower. The defenders tried to countermine at the Tower of the Countess of Blois and 'fought back fiercely' but were clearly outnumbered in this aspect of the siege.

The Westerners' almost complete command of the sea enabled ships to bring supplies and reinforcements into Acre, weather permitting, and allowed the defenders to land raiding parties. Ships or barges could also be used as floating batteries, an area in which the Pisans were particularly skilled. On the night of 13–14 April several ships, including one with a mangonel on board, approached the shore north of Montmusard. A landing party harassed the Hama army and next day the

mangonel bombarded their camp. In response the Muslims could only shoot at the ships because their own mangonels were facing the fortifications of Acre. Fortunately a storm blew up and the Crusaders' ships were so tossed about that their mangonel broke and was not repaired.

The defenders next launched large-scale sorties against the Mamluk siege lines. The first was on the night of 15–16 April through the Gate of St Lazarus when the Templars, led by Guillaume de Beaujeu, were joined by Othon de Grandson, probably at the head of the Order of St Thomas, and perhaps the leper Order of St Lazarus. Their target was again the Hama contingent and, according to the Templar of Tyre:

> The Master ordered a Provençal, who was the viscount of the bourg of
> Acre, to set fire to the wooden buches of the great engine of the sultan.
> They went out that night, and came up to these buches, but the man
> who was supposed to hurl the Greek Fire was afraid when he threw it,
> and it fell short and landed on the ground where it burned out…. Our

RELATIVES OF THOSE MASSACRED BY THE CRUSADERS IN ACRE DEMONSTRATING IN A CAIRO MOSQUE (pages 62–63)
Relatives of those killed by newly arrived Crusaders in Acre travelled to Cairo, and survivors including Syrian merchants (1) and Palestinian peasants (2) showed the bloodstained clothes of the dead. They demanded that the Mamluk Sultan take action. At first they would have spoken to ordinary people during communal prayers in the main mosques, but soldiers (3), government employees (4) and members of the Mamluk ruling elite (5) would soon have reported these events to the Sultan. This had long been a traditional method of influencing an Islamic government and it was again effective, especially as Sultan Qalawun may have been looking for an excuse to launch a final assault upon Acre. Since the records do not mention which particular mosques were involved, the building shown here is based upon the interiors or covered prayer-halls of several early Mamluk mosques. These included the obligatory mihrab niche (6) which indicated the direction of prayer facing Mecca, the minbar or preaching pulpit (7), and in many cases also a raised platform which could be used for preaching or private study (8). (Graham Turner)

men, both brethren and secular knights, went so far in amongst the tents that their horses got their legs tangled in the tent ropes and went sprawling, whereupon the Saracens slew them. In this way we lost eighteen horsemen that night... though they did capture a number of Saracen shields and bucklers and trumpets and drums.

One unfortunate Crusader fell into an *amir's* latrine where he was killed. The following day, the men of Hama presented Sultan Khalil with several captured horses which had the heads of slain enemies hanging from their saddles. In turn, the defenders displayed the captured shields and armours on the walls of Acre. The *Chronicle of Lanercost* claimed that 5,000 prisoners were taken; probably a misunderstanding reflecting the fact that so many Muslim slaves were already held in Acre. Other sorties that same night failed because the enemy was already alerted.

A second attempt on the night of the 18th–19th aimed at the centre of the Mamluk line where the Syrian provincial contingents met the Sultan's army from Egypt. The Hospitallers took the leading role, supported by some Templars but, as the Templar of Tyre wrote: 'This was decided so secretly that no one knew of it until the command "To horse!" was given. At the time when our men mounted up and sallied forth from the Gate of St Anthony, the moon was not shining at all, but was obscured. The Saracens were forewarned, and illuminated the scene with torches so that it seemed to be day along their lines. The Mamluks counterattacked and the Crusaders withdrew, many of their horses being wounded.'

According to the *Chronicle of Lanercost*, probably based upon the recollections of Othon de Grandson, he and the Templars planned another attempt for Good Friday, 20 April; 'with their captives massed as a screen before them,' but this use of prisoners as a human screen was banned by the Patriarch 'acting on the advice of traitors.' Al-Yusufi wrote that the Mamluks were warned of one sortie by a secret convert to Islam inside Acre who shot an arrow with a message tied to it. It was directed against the Mamluks' left flank 'from the sea', but the warning enabled Badr al-Din Bektash al-Fakhri, the Templar Grand Master's supposed spy,

THE FAILURE OF THE INITIAL MAMLUK ATTACKS (15 April to night 15/16 May 1291)

(Note: The medieval sea level was 2 metres lower than today)

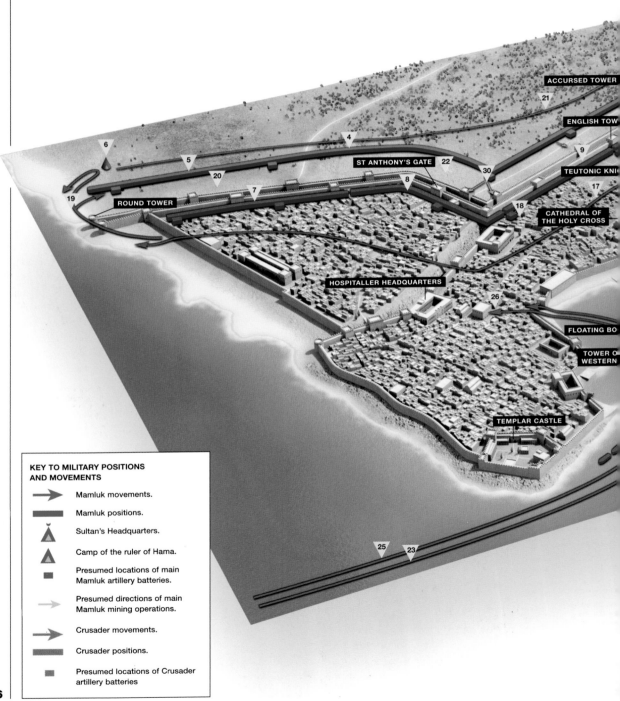

ACCURSED TOWER
21

ENGLISH TOW
9

TEUTONIC KNI
17

CATHEDRAL OF
THE HOLY CROSS

6

5

4

ST ANTHONY'S GATE 22

30

20

7

8

18

19

ROUND TOWER

HOSPITALLER HEADQUARTERS

26

FLOATING BO

TOWER O
WESTERN

TEMPLAR CASTLE

25   23

KEY TO MILITARY POSITIONS AND MOVEMENTS

→ Mamluk movements.

▬ Mamluk positions.

⛺ Sultan's Headquarters.

⛺ Camp of the ruler of Hama.

▪ Presumed locations of main Mamluk artillery batteries.

→ Presumed directions of main Mamluk mining operations.

→ Crusader movements.

▬ Crusader positions.

▪ Presumed locations of Crusader artillery batteries

EVENTS

Sultan Khalil's HQ on Tal al-Fukhar.

Mamluk army of Egypt facing the fortifications of Acre proper, from the Bay of Acre to the junction with the fortifications of Montmusard.

3 **Karak contingent commanded by Baybars al-Mansuri stationed opposite the salient formed by the junction of Acre's northern and eastern walls.**

4 **Syrian contingent under Husam al-Din Lajin al-Mansuri, the governor of Damascus, face the eastern and northern fortifications of Montmusard.**

5 **The army of the Ayyubid vassal-ruler of Hama, al-Malik al-Muzaffar, on the right wing of the Mamluk line.**

6 **The camp of al-Muzaffar and his army behind the siege lines, probably between the beach and a coastal marsh.**

7 **Templars man walls and towers along the northern fortifications of Montmusard.**

8 **Hospitallers man walls and towers along the eastern fortifications of Montmusard.**

9 **Teutonic Knights probably man walls and towers between the Hospitallers and the troops of King Henry II.**

10A-B **The King's troops of Cyprus and the Kingdom of Jerusalem man the north-eastern corner of Acre proper, and probably the barbican ahead of the King's Tower.**

11 **French Crusaders under Jean de Grailly.**

12 **English Crusaders under Othon de Grandson.**

KING'S TOWER

TOWER OF FLIES AT THE END OF COLLAPSED MOLE

13 **Venetian troops and militia, probably including Italian Crusaders.**

14 **Pisan troops and militia.**

15 **Urban militia of Acre.**

16 **Possible location of the munitions stores for Mamluk mangonels.**

17 **Perhaps one of the munitions stores for Crusader Mangonels.**

18 **Othon de Grandson, probably accompanied by the Order of St Thomas, joins the Templar sortie against the western flank of the Mamluk lines.**

19 **A substantial Templar force launches a surprise sortie against the Hama army; the Crusaders reach the Hama camp but their horses are impeded by tent guy-ropes; the Crusaders suffer heavy casualties (15-16 April).**

20 **Crusaders display captured shields and armour on the walls of Acre (16 April).**

21 **Sultan Khalis is presented with captured enemy horses, the heads of dead Crusaders hanging from their necks (16 April).**

22 **A night sortie by the Hospitallers, reportedly supported by some Templars, through St Anthony's Gate is unsuccessful (probably night of 18-19 April).**

23 **The Christians had almost complete control of the sea, enabling ships to bring food and munitions from Cyprus.**

24 **Templars attempt a sortie 'from the sea' against the left flank of the mamluk lines, but this is ambushed by Fakhr al-Din Bektash (probably on 20 April).**

25 **Henry II arrives in Acre from Cyprus with his army of about 100 cavalry and about 2,000 infantry in forty ships (4 May).**

26 **Celebrations in Acre at the arrival of the King, with bonfires being lit in his honour; the King takes command of the defence.**

27 **Henry II sends a peace delegation consisting of the Templar William de Cafran and a knight named William de Villiers, to meet Sultan Khalil; both sides are ordered not to shoot at the enemy while negotiations are in progress (probably 7 May).**

28 **Sultan Khalil and his attendants meet the Crusader peace delegation outside the Gate of the Legate.**

29 **Discussions continue until a stone from a Crusader mangonel lands close to the Sultan; the talks end acrimoniously.**

30 **The King's troops abandon the barbican ahead of the King's Tower; this is set on fire and left to collapse (8 May).**

31 **The English Tower, the Tower of the Countess of Blois, the walls of St Anthony's Gate and those next to the Tower of St Nicholas begin to crumble as a result of Mamluk mining and mangonel bombardment (8 to 15 May).**

32 **Sultan Khalil arrests Husam al-Din Lajin and his supporters on suspicion of treachery (probably on 9 May).**

33 **Part of the outer wall of the King's Tower collapses (15 May).**

32 **Baybars al-Mansuri's men erect a felt screen during the night, enabling Mamluk sappers to construct an access path to the King's Tower across the ruins (night of 15-16 May).**

Old Acre is still a largely Palestinian Arab town, which is why it retains a bustling character similar to that which could have been seen before the city fell to the Mamluks in 1291. (Author's photograph)

to ambush the attackers and capture several. Was Badr al-Din a double-agent or did he realize that the Crusader cause was lost. Certainly Sultan Khalil did not trust all his senior officers and, after berating the *amirs* for not trying hard enough, he arrested Husam al-Din Lajin and his supporters around 9 May. Amongst them was Badr al-Din Bektash who was at the time Lajin's household steward.

Inside Acre people lost heart, though they hoped King Henry II could still save the day. He arrived from Famagusta on 4 May, with forty ships, 100 knights and 2,000 infantrymen to assume command of the defence. Henry had been ill but he was now received with hysterical enthusiasm. Whatever his other failings, the young king was a realist and soon concluded that a negotiated peace was the only hope. Three days later Henry sent the Templar William of Cafran and another knight named William of Villiers to meet Sultan Khalil, both sides agreeing not to shoot while negotiations were in progress. In the words of the Templar of Tyre; 'he (the Sultan) approached them and said, "Have you brought me the keys of the city?"' In recognition of young King Henry's courage, despite his illness, the Mamluks would spare the people if Acre immediately surrendered. The ambassadors pointed out that they would be accused of treachery if they agreed without consultation, while a great shout from the *suqa* (rabble), *harafish* (vagabonds), *ghilman* (mamluk soldiers) and *jamalin* (camel drivers) demanded that the siege continue. So Khalil dismissed the ambassadors, but; 'As he spoke these words, there was a siege engines that the Crusaders were working from the Gate of the Legate, and it shot by

When Acre was rebuilt in the later Ottoman period, the ruins of the medieval city were levelled, burying several substantial Crusader structures. Some have since been excavated, including the courtyard of the Citadel. (Author's photograph)

Until it was excavated a few years ago, the undercroft of the Crusader Citadel was filled with rubble to within a metre of its roof. (Author's photograph)

I know not what accident, and the stone came so near the tent where the sultan and his messengers were.'

Khalil was furious and threatened to kill the ambassadors, but was dissuaded by Sanjar al-Shuja'i. Instead they were allowed to return safely to Acre, where morale now collapsed. As many as 3,000 members of the Crusader aristocracy fled before the city fell. Most of the Italian merchant communes fought to the end, though many Venetians sailed to safety. On 8 May the barbican in front of the King's Tower was abandoned, probably due to mining, the defenders setting it on fire and retreating inside the King's Tower. Sanjar al-Shuja'i's troops facing this sector edged cautiously forwards. During the following week the English Tower, the Tower of the Countess of Blois, the walls of St Anthony's Gate and those next to the Tower of St Nicholas all began to crumble. A Crusader attempt to countermine near the King's Tower failed and may have contributed to the collapse of its outer wall on 15 May.

The fallen masonry was too jumbled for the Muslims to make an assault but the following night Baybars al-Mansuri, commander of the Karak contingent, had his men make a long felt screen, as he later recalled in his memoirs: 'Between two posts opposite the dilapidated tower I placed a pulley rigged with ropes similar to a ship's. There I hoisted the felt into place like a dam. This was done under the wing of night, unknown to the people of Acre who, when they rose in the morning and saw the screen, shot mangonels and arrows against it.' These had no effect whatsoever and behind their screen Baybars' men made a path along which the Sultan's army could storm the damaged tower.

The Templar of Tyre saw this work from the other side; 'The Saracens made small sacks of hemp cloth and filled them with sand. Every man carried one of these sacks on the neck of his horse and tossed it to the Saracens who were there behind the *buches* at that point. Then when night fell, they took the sacks and spread them across the top of the stones, and smoothed them out like a road.' Having built ramparts to protect their *carabohas*, the Mamluks attacked next morning and captured the ruined tower, despite being shot at by the defenders' siege

69

CRUSADER SHIPS ATTACK THE RIGHT FLANK OF THE MAMLUK SIEGE CAMP (pages 72–73)
A week after the beginning of the Mamluk siege of Acre a merchant ship (1) was towed from Acre harbour into a position close to the right flank of the Mamluk siege lines. It was accompanied by several other ships (2 & 3) and, the following morning, as a stone-throwing mangonel (4) on the merchant ship bombarded the Sultan of Hama's army (5), men from other vessels attacked with arrows and crossbows (6) while yet others went ashore (7), raiding the poorly defended rear areas behind the Mamluk lines. All the troops from Hama could do in response was to shoot arrows at the ships, because their own stone-throwing mangonels were positioned to bombard the walls of Acre. (Graham Turner)

engines; 'When our men saw that the tower was taken, they built a structure out of leather-covered wood, called a *chat*, and put men inside it, so that the Saracens who had taken the tower might not advance further.' Meanwhile other Mamluk forces attacked St Anthony's Gate, probably as a diversion. Here Matthew de Clermont, Marshal of the Hospitallers, was distinguished by his bravery, but the Accursed Tower, behind the lost King's Tower, was now the key to the defence of Acre.

On 17 May the women and children who had carried food and water to the men defending the walls of Acre were sent home. Others, probably from prosperous families, went aboard the available ships but a storm blew up and those who could not endure it returned home.

THE CITY FALLS

Accounts of the fall of Acre offer differing versions of who fought well on the last day, and who did not. *De Exidio Urbis Acconis* claimed that Jean de Grailly and Othon de Grandson fled to their ships before the final assault while most other sources claim that both were heroes. The *Historia Sicula* by De Neocastro accuses the Papal Crusaders of indulging in wine and women even as the trumpet sounded but the Templar of Tyre described how Italian Crusaders from Spoloto fought in the last battle around the Accursed Tower.

The Mamluks extended their control as far as possible along the outer wall while beyond Acre's fortifications Sultan Khalil told his troops to prepare for a final assault. Before sunrise on Friday 18 May the Egyptian army advanced to the base of the walls, then surged forward against the fortification from the Patriarch's Tower to St Anthony's Gate.

Running beneath much of the south-western part of Acre is the so-called "secret tunnel of the Templars" which is now partially flooded by the risen sea level. (Author's photograph)

THE MAMLUK BREAK-IN AND THE FALL OF THE CITY (16 May to 28 May 1291)

(Note: The medieval sea level was 2 metres lower than today)

▼ EVENTS

1 **Sultan Khalil's HQ on Tal al-Fukhar.**

2 **Original position of the Mamluk army of Egypt facing the fortifications of Acre proper, from the Bay of Acre to the junction with the fortifications of Montmusard.**

3 **Original position of the Karak contingent commanded by Baybars al-Mansuri, stationed opposite the salient formed by the junction of Acre's northern and eastern walls.**

4 **Original position of the Syrian contingent under Husam al-Din Lajin al-Mansuri facing the eastern and northern fortifications of Montmusard.**

5 **Original position of the army of the Ayyubid vassal-ruler of Hama, al-Malik al-Muzaffar, on the right wing of the Mamluk line.**

6 **The camp of al-Muzaffar and his army behind the siege lines, probably between the beach and a coastal marsh.**

7 **Templars man walls and towers along the northern fortifications of Montmusard.**

ACCURSED TO

ENGLISH TOWER

ST ANTHONY'S GATE

ROUND TOWER

TEUTONIC KN

CATHEDRAL OF THE HOLY CROS

HOSPITALLER HEADQUARTERS

FLOATING BO

TOWER O WESTERN

TEMPLAR CASTLE

KEY TO MILITARY POSITIONS AND MOVEMENTS

→ Mamluk movements.

▬ Mamluk positions.

Ⱥ Sultan's Headquarters.

Ⱥ Camp of the ruler of Hama.

▬ Presumed locations of main Mamluk artillery batteries.

→ Presumed directions of main Mamluk mining operations.

→ Crusader movements.

▬ Crusader positions.

▬ Presumed locations of Crusader artillery batteries.

21 **Mamluk units take control of much of the outer wall (17 May).**

22 **Sultan Khalil orders the army to prepare for a general assault on the following morning (17 May).**

23 **The Sultan's Army advances to the base of the walls then attacks the entire length from the Patriarch's Tower to St Anthony's Gate (before sunrise on 18 May).**

24 **The main Mamluk effort is directed against the Accursed Tower at the northeastern angle of the walls of Acre proper; this is soon taken.**

25 **The King's troops retreat along the northern walls of Acre.**

26 **Templars and Hospitallers move to support the King's troops.**

27 **Matthew de Clermont, Marshal of the Hospitallers, leads an attempt to retake the Accursed Tower, followed by the Grand Masters of the Templars and the Hospitallers; this attempt fails and Guillaume de Beaujeu, Grand Master of the Templars, is mortally wounded, while the Grand Master of the Hospitallers is also injured (early morning 18 May).**

Hospitallers man walls and towers along the
eastern fortifications of Montmusard.

Teutonic Knights probably man walls and
towers between the Hospitallers and the
troops of King Henry II.

10 **The King's troops of Cyprus and the
Kingdom of Jerusalem man the salient at the
north-eastern corner of Acre proper, but have
abandoned the barbican ahead of the King's
Tower.**

11 **French Crusaders under Jean de Grailly.**

12 **English Crusaders under Othon de
Grandson.**

13 **Venetian troops and militia, perhaps
including Italian Crusaders.**

14 **Pisan troops and militia.**

15 **Urban militia of Acre.**

16 **Mamluk troops advance under the cover of
to take over the ruined King's Tower (morning
of 16 May).**

17 **The Crusader defenders are driven from
the King's Tower to the inner wall where the
Accursed Tower becomes the key defensive
position (morning of 16 May).**

18 **Mamluk forces from Syria launch a major
attack on the damaged St Anthony's Gate but
are defeated(16 May).**

19 **Hospitallers and Templars join forces
to defeat the attack on St Anthony's Gate;
Matthew de Clermont, the Marshal of the
Hospitallers, particularly distinguishes himself
(16 May).**

20 **Women and children are ordered to return
to their homes due to imminent Mamluk
assault (morning of 17 May).**

TOWER

28
33
13
12
14
2
1
23

TOWER OF FLIES AT THE END
OF COLLAPSED MOLE

28 **French and English Crusaders under Jean
de Grailly and Othon de Grandson defend the
eastern walls of Acre for several hours but are
forced southwards until the Tower of St
Nicholas is taken by Mamluk troops.**

29 **The Templar Grand Master is taken to the
Order's HQ where he dies.**

30 **Matthew de Clermont accompanies the
Templar Grand Master but returns to the
fighting after the Grand Master dies.**

31 **The wounded Grand Master of the
Hospitallers is taken to the harbour by his
attendants where he is put in a boat.**

32 **King Henry II and his brother Amalric board
a ship.**

33 **Jean de Grailly is wounded and Othon de
Grandson takes command of the eastern wall.**

34 **Othon de Grandson orders the Venetians
and perhaps the Pisans to assemble ships.
Jean de Grailly and other wounded are put on
board. Othon de Grandson goes to the
Templar headquarters.**

35 **Confusion and panic as people crowd into
boats; many are drowned as overloaded
vessels sink. Some ships' captains demand
large sums to take them to Cyprus.**

36 **Much of the population of Acre and
Montmusard hide in their houses until the
chaos subsides.**

37 **The Sultan's army is reportedly in effective
control of Acre within three hours of the initial
assault; there is widespread killing and looting
before order is restored.**

38 **The role of the Mamluk forces of Syria and
of Ayyubid Hama is unclear; they probably
entered Montmusard after many of its Templar
and Hospitaller defenders had been sent to
support those defending the eastern part of
the city (late on 18 May).**

39 **Sultan Khalil sends troops to blockade Tyre
(19 May).**

40 **Surviving Teutonic Knights retreat to their
headquarters where they are besieged by
Mamluk troops; 'two days after the fall of the
city' they ask for an amnesty. This is granted
by the Sultan (probably 20 May).**

41 **Surviving Hospitallers retreat to their headquarters where they are besieged by Mamluk
troops; 'two days after the fall of the city' they
ask for an amnesty. This is granted by the
Sultan (probably 20 May).**

42 **Surviving Templars retreat to their headquarters where they are besieged by Mamluk
troops; 'two days after the fall of the city' they
ask for amnesty. This is granted by the
Sultan. However, some Mamluks are accused
of molesting civilians in the building; the
Templars close their gates and kill most of the
Muslims trapped inside; the siege continues
(probably 20 May).**

43 **Some ships returning from Cyprus deliver
food to those in the Templar fortress and take
some people back to Cyprus.**

44 **The Marshal of the Templars, Peter de
Sevrey, sends the Order's Treasury and its
Commander, Tibald Gaudin, to Sidon (perhaps
the night of 25-26 May).**

The Mamluks' main effort was against the Accursed Tower defended by King Henry II's own troops from Acre and Cyprus, while those manning the outer wall were forced back towards St Anthony's Gate. The Mamluks reportedly had 300 camel-mounted drummers but the Templar of Tyre noted one particularly terrible instrument:

> Before dawn on the next day, Friday, a drum began a powerful stroke and at the sound of this drum, which had a horrible and mighty voice, the Saracens assailed the city of Acre upon all sides. The place where they entered first was by the Accursed Tower. ... In front came men carrying great tall shields, and after them came men who threw Greek Fire, and after them came men who hurled javelins and shot feathered arrows ... . Our men who were inside the chat abandoned it. At this the Saracens ... took two routes, since they were between the two walls of the city .... Some of them entered by a gate of that great tower called the Accursed Tower, and moved towards San Romano where the Pisans had their great engines. The others kept to the (main) road, going to St Anthony's Gate.

In this crisis the Military Orders attempted to retake the Accursed Tower. Their counterattack was led by Matthew de Clermont, followed by the Grand Masters of the Hospitallers and Templars. According to the *De Exidio Urbis Acconis*, Jean de Villiers and Matthew de Clermont shouted at fugitives in the streets, 'Shame upon you! Fools, you are not hurt! To the battle with you, by the Faith of Christ!' The Templar of Tyre focused on the Templars' role:

> Those of the enemy who were hurling Greek Fire hurled it so often and so thickly that there was so much smoke that one man could scarcely see another. Amongst the smoke, archers shot feathered arrows so densely that our men and mounts were terribly hurt. It happened that one poor English valet (military servant) was so badly hit by the Greek Fire... that his surcoat burst into flames. There was no one to help him, and so his face was burned, and then his whole body, and he burned as if he had been a cauldron of pitch and he died there.... The Saracens hung back for a bit, then raised their shields and moved forwards a little ways, and when our men charged down upon them, they straightway fixed all their shields and drew together.

Jean de Villiers described the collapse of resistance in a letter he later wrote from Cyprus:

> Meanwhile a great crowd of Saracens were entering the city on all sides, by land and by sea. Moving along the walls, which were all pierced and broken, until they came to our shelters.... We and our brothers, the greatest number of whom were wounded to death or gravely injured, resisted them as long as we could, God knows.... And as some of us were lying as if half-dead and lay in a faint before our enemies, our sergeants and our household boys came and carried me, gravely wounded, and our brothers away, at great danger to themselves.

Jean de Villiers had been struck by a spear between his shoulders, a wound which, he noted, 'made the writing of this letter very difficult.'

At the south-western tip of Acre there is an area of shallow water which had formed part of the Templar quarter of the fortified city of Acre. (Author's photograph)

The Grand Master of the Templars was mortally wounded, as the Templar of Tyre described: 'A javelin came at the Master of the Temple, just as he raised his left hand. He had no shield save his staff in his right hand, and the javelin struck him under the armpit, and the shaft sank into his body a palm's depth. It came in through the gap where the plates of the armour were not joined. This was not his proper armour, but rather light armour for putting on hastily at an alarm.' The wounded Master turned to go and the standard bearer followed, so everyone thought they were retreating. 'Twenty Crusaders from the Valle di Spoleto saw him withdrawing, and they called to him, "Oh for God's sake, Sir, do not leave or the city will fall at once!"'

Guillaume de Beaujeu's bodyguards carried the Grand Master towards St Anthony's Gate but it was closed, indicating that the counter-attack had been launched between the inner and outer walls. Fortunately they found a door with a bridge leading from the moat into the palace of Princess Maria of Antioch. After removing the Grand Master's cuirass, his servants carried him to the harbour, where they learned that the Mamluks had also broken through the eastern wall. Unable to reach the small boats because the water was so rough, they next took Guillaume de Beaujeu to the Templar Castle, 'but not going in the main gate because they did not want to open this, but via a courtyard where they piled manure.' The Hospitaller Matthew de Clermont remained with the Templar Grand Master until the latter died, then returned to the increasingly hopeless fight where Matthew was killed in a final desperate stand by several Hospitaller knights in a square in the Genoese quarter.

On the eastern wall the Italian communal militias, plus the English and French under Othon de Grandson and Jean de Grailly respectively, continued to resist after the loss of the Accursed Tower. But when other Mamluks broke through along the shoreline their position became untenable, as the Templar of Tyre recorded: 'From the edge of the sea to the foot of the tower the Saracens prised off a lattice-work which had bars and points sticking out so that horses could not get through there. Then a great number of mounted Saracens

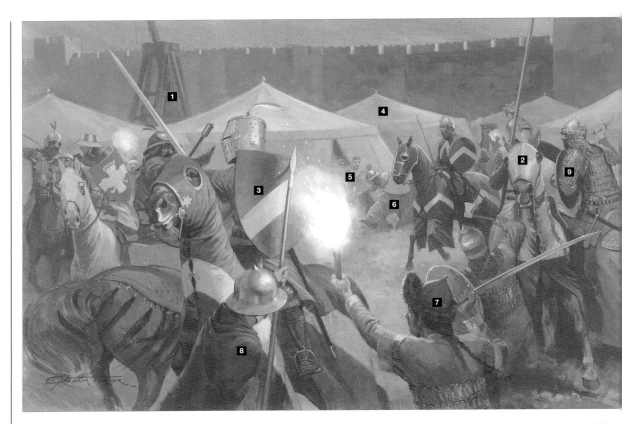

**UNSUCCESSFUL NIGHTIME SORTIE BY THE CRUSADER
DEFENDERS OF ACRE, NIGHT 15 APRIL** (pages 78–79)
At Acre, the defenders had complete command of the
sea, so their sorties would have been intended solely to
damage the enemy's siege lines and artillery (1). The most
successful sortie was on the night of 15th-16th April when
a substantial force of Templars (2), supported by secular
knights (3) led by Othon de Grandson and perhaps the
English Military Order of St. Thomas, attacked the camp (4)
of the army of Hama which they caught by surprise and
often ready for bed (5). But when the Crusaders reached the
Hama camp their horses were impeded and in some cases
tripped up (6) by tents and guy-ropes. This gave the Muslim
time to recover and gather those pickets and sentries who
were already armed. The army of Hama included a variety
of troops, including Turks (7) and local Syrians (8). There
may also have been members of the Mamluk elite present
(9). As a result the Crusader sortie suffered heavy losses,
though they did capture some of the Muslims' equipment.
(Graham Turner)

came in. Sir Jean de Grailly and Sir Othon de Grandson and the men of the King of France put up a fierce defence, so that there were many wounded and dead.' Jean de Grailly was amongst those injured and other sources indicate that Othon de Grandson now took over. His men commandeered some Venetian ships, put Jean de Grailly and the other wounded on board, then fell back to the Templar Castle.

Arabic sources focused upon the chaos and carnage in Acre which, having been taken by the sword, could expect no mercy. In the words of Abu'l-Mahasin, 'The Franks cast themselves into the sea, trampled on by the Muslim troops who killed and captured them. Only a few escaped.' The Templar of Tyre was more specific: 'For the Saracens, as I have said, had come through the Accursed Tower and went straight through San Romano and set fire to the great engine of the Pisans, and went down the straight road to the Germans (the Convent of the Teutonic Knights).... The Saracens set fire to the siege engines and to the *garites* (moveable wooden defences) so that the whole land was lit up by the flames.' He also recorded that some Muslim soldiers were so appalled at the sight of children who had been trampled and killed in the panic that, 'as we learned afterwards, they had pity on these victims and wept.'

Things were similarly desperate at the harbour where there were not enough boats to take even those who had money to pay. So huge crowds sought refuge in the fortified Templar complex. By nightfall Acre was firmly in the hands of the Mamluks, except for the fortified convents of the three main Military Orders and perhaps the Citadel. The Mamluk provincial forces of Syria and the Ayyubid army of Hama probably broke into Montmusard after the Hospitallers and Templars sent troops to try and retake the Accursed Tower. The defenders may have fallen back to the Citadel and the old northern wall of Acre proper, though this is not recorded in the sources. The leper Order of St Lazarus defending Montmusard were all slain. Their leader, Thomas de Sainville, survived, which probably means he was not present when Acre fell.

Meanwhile King Henry and Jean de Villiers, the wounded Hospitaller Grand Master, realized that the city was lost, so they gathered their remaining men and sailed to Cyprus. The wounded Jean de Grailly also left 'with the king'. There are two versions of the drowning of the wounded Patriach of Jerusalem, Nicholas de Hanape. One says that he fell when trying to board a ship; the other that he was put aboard a small boat but allowed too many fugitives to accompany him, causing the vessel to capsize.

The behaviour of some ships' captains was not particularly honourable. Roger de Flor commanded a large Templar ship and charged large sums of money from those he saved. He was subsequently pursued by the

Templars who accused him of keeping some of the money for himself, after which Roger de Flor became leader of the notorious Catalan Grand Company of mercenaries.

Many of the supposedly money-minded Italian merchants behaved better and the Templar of Tyre even praised the widely criticized Genoese who, as he wrote, 'did much good as everyone knows, for they collected the men from the seashore and put them in the *nefs* (large sailing ships) and on the other *leins* (large galleys). The commander of these two galleys was a Genoese named Andrea Peleau.' Some of the poor tried to swim to the larger ships, a few being fished out of the water by the Genoese. Then, as the big ships raised their sails and headed for Cyprus a great cry went up from the thousands crammed into the Templar Castle.

Sultan Khalil had already sent a reconnaissance detachment under 'Alam al-Din Sanjar al-Sawabi to blockade Tyre, in the correct assumption that when the Crusaders lost Acre they would try to reinforce Tyre. Over a century earlier Saladin was widely, though not entirely fairly, blamed for allowing the Crusaders to do just that, and Khalil was not going make the same strategic error.

On 20 May three of the four 'lofty towers' inside Acre surrendered on terms. The first to 'ask for amnesty', as the Arabic sources put it, was the fortified convent of the Hospitallers, soon followed by that of the Teutonic Knights. Both seem to have been handed over to an *amir*, Zain al-Din Kitbugha al-Mansuri. The fact that there were many Armenian troops in the Hospitallers' 'tower' probably reflected the close links between the Hospitallers and the Armenian Kingdom of Cilician. The third 'tower' is unidentified but may have been the Citadel where some of King Henry's troops probably retreated.

Next a Mamluk representative went to the Templar fortress which, unlike the others, could not be entirely surrounded. According to the Chronicle of St Peter's in Erfurt, written later in the summer of 1291 before news of the fall of Sidon and 'Atlit reached Germany; 'It is said that a good 7,000 (other sources say 10,000) people fled to the house of the Templars. Because it was located in a strong part of the city, over-looking the sea shore, and was surrounded by good walls.' The Templar of Tyre explained how it could reasonably have hoped to withstand the Mamluks even after the city fell.

It occupied a large site on the sea, like a castle. It had at its entry a tall, strong tower and the wall was thick, twenty-eight feet wide. At each corner of the tower was a turret and upon each turret was a gilded lion passant, as big as a donkey... And on the other corner, towards the Pisan quarter, there was another tower, and near this tower above the street of St Ann there was a most noble palace which belonged to the Master. Opposite this the house of the nuns of St Anne had a high tower in which were bells and there was a most noble and tall church. The Templar fortress also had another very old tower, on the sea, which Saladin had built a hundred years before, in which the Templars kept their treasure. It was so close to the sea that the waves broke against it.

Nevertheless, the Templars also requested an amnesty, but when some Mamluk *amirs* and their troops arrived things got out of hand, as the chronicler Abu'l-Mahasin wrote:

He (the Sultan) sent them a banner which they accepted and raised over the tower. When the door was opened a crowd of soldiers and others swarmed in. When they came face to face with the defenders, some of the soldiers began to pillage and to lay hands on the women and children who were there, whereupon the Franks shut the door and attacked them, killing a number of Muslims. They hauled down the banner and stiffened their resistance.

The Templar of Tyre confirmed that the unit which was sent to accept the surrender of the fortress included 400 horsemen.

An anonymous Muslim who survived later described his adventure:

The Sultan granted them amnesty through his envoys, the amir Sayf al-Din Baktamur al-Silahdar, Aylik al-Farisi al-Hajib (the secretary), the amir Sayf al-Din Aqbugha al-Mansuri al-Silahdar who was martyred in this tower, and Ibn al-Qadi Taqi al-Din Ibn Razin, who were to administer an oath to the Franks and evacuate them under safe conduct. But the rapacious throng fell upon them and killed one of the envoys (Sayf al-Din Aqbugha). Thereupon the Franks closed the gates and expelled the Muslims. When the tumult first broke out, the amirs left and thereby saved their lives. I, along with a companion named Qarabugha al-Shukri were among the group who went to the tower, and when the gates were closed we remained inside with many others. The Franks killed many people and then came to the place where a small number, including my companions and me, had taken refuge. We fought them for an hour, and most of our number, including my comrade, were killed. But I escaped with a group of ten persons who fled from them. Being outnumbered, we hurled ourselves into the sea. Some died, some were crippled, and some of us were spared for a time.

It was probably at this point that those who had found refuge in the Templar castle massacred the prisoners whom the Templars had hoped to use as bargaining chips in their negotiations with Sultan Khalil. For this the Mamluks blamed the Templars.

Some days later, on 25 or 26 May, the Marshal of the Templars, Peter de Sevrey, sent the Order's Treasury and some non-combatants to Cyprus in ships that had returned from Cyprus. Othon de Grandson probably also left, and a later slander accused him of fleeing under an assumed name and taking the Templars' treasure for his own use. In reality Othon de Grandson arrived in Cyprus destitute and ten years later the Pope ordered the Dean of St Paul's to pay him 3,000 marks in compensation.

On 28 May Sultan Khalil offered the same terms as before. Peter de Sevrey and some companions emerged to discuss the surrender but were promptly executed in retaliation for the killing of Sayf al-Din Aqbugha and the prisoners. In response the defenders threw five more Muslim captives from a tower, though one survived. Mamluk miners now undermined the building and its landward fortifications crumbled; a Mamluk force stormed the breach and virtually all the adult men found inside were killed while women and children were taken captive. According to Abu'l-Mahasin, 'When the Franks had come out and most of the contents had been removed, the tower collapsed on a group of sightseers and on the looters inside, killing them all.' Not surprisingly, the Templars' last stand became an epic in the eyes of Christian Europe and events were steadily embroidered, with the collapse of the fortifications becoming an heroic finale in which the last defenders and their foes died together beneath the ruins.

The fate of those who did not escape Acre also became the stuff of legend, though the reality was bad enough. A Dominican friar named Ricoldo de Monte Croce had travelled via Acre, Tripoli and Tartus on his way to Baghdad, but had paused between Erzerum and Mosul to learn Arabic. He was still there when he heard about the fall of Acre, and in a letter written fours weeks after the event Ricoldo reported that no less than 30,000 Christians had been killed in Acre. A member of the clergy who had been taken as a slave told him that thirty preaching friars of his own Dominican Order had refused to flee and had been joined by a large number of friars Minor – all then being slaughtered while saying Mass.

This was probably true, but a later 14th-century story about heroic nuns who had cut off their own noses to make themselves so ugly that the Mamluks would not want to rape them was also certainly fictitious. On the other hand, the victorious Muslims may well have been shocked by what they would have seen as any undue fanaticism on the part of captured Christian women since, according to Islamic law, women were not expected to save their honour by death and no blame resulted if they survived by having sex with a conqueror. In fact, Ricoldo de Monte Croce reported that some nuns captured at Acre ended up in the harems of *amirs* or officers. He tried to ransom fellow Dominican friars but found none, though he did manage to buy some looted religious objects and relics, including a breviary which had been pierced with a spear and splashed with blood. The most precious books Ricoldo saved were a *Moralia of St Gregory* and a missal.

The number of members of the Military Orders who were captured and survived the fall of Acre is surprising. The prospects of their ransom were worse than those seized in earlier years, but the Sultan clearly used the release of prisoners as a bargaining counter and as a source of favourable propaganda, not that such releases were always approved of. In 1294 the chief Hanafi *qadi* religious judge in Damascus wrote a poem criticizing the Governor for releasing a Christian who had harmed Islam: 'You (*mamluks*) who are lions in the Holy War, You are the sword of God in the land of Syria, If you do not succour the Faith, There will be nobody to repel those who attack it.' That same year the Templar Brother Knight Hugh d'Empúries, captured at the fall of Tripoli, was ransomed after King James of Sicily sent a letter to the Sultan. Other Catalan Templars and Hospitallers captured at Acre were released after fifteen years, including Brothers Lope de Linares and Guillem de Villalba plus ten squires and servants. Other Templars who were never released were seen by the German pilgrim Ludolphe de Suchem living as aged woodcutters near the Dead Sea in 1340. Most of the Templars captured at Acre, and probably members of the other Military Orders, eventually converted to Islam. One such was a knight named Pierre who was an interpreter in the Sultan's service in 1323.

The only record of Islamic casualties at the siege of Acre suggests an incredibly low figure. However, the list of seven *amirs* or senior officers, excluding the *amir* killed in the Templar fortress, plus six commanders of the *halqa* freeborn troops, thirty *amirs'* troops meaning *mamluks*, and fifty-three *halqa* soldiers is possible if the only soldiers to be included were members of the professional, regularly paid élite listed by the Mamluk government's *diwan al-jaysh* or Ministry of War. Most of the soldiers who took part in the siege were not members of this élite while non-military volunteers reportedly outnumbered all forms of soldier. No record survives of the losses suffered by either such group.

AFTERMATH

On 18 March 1291, as the siege of Acre got under way, Pope Nicholas IV in Rome issued the final approval for King Edward of England's Crusade. Edward would set out on 24 June, by which time Acre had, of course, already fallen and the plan was aborted.

Margaret of Tyre had handed her city over to Amalaric of Cyprus a few months before the siege of Acre, by which time it only had a tiny garrison. Sultan Khalil sent a small unit under 'Alam al-Din Sanjar al-Sawabi to Tyre even before Acre fell and the defenders reportedly started evacuating when they saw the smoke of fallen Acre in the distance. On 22 May ships from Acre appeared off Tyre, but the Mamluks prevented them entering the harbour. That same day the Sultan sent siege engineers under Sayf al-Din Ibn al-Mihaffadar and Sayf al-Din Qutuz al-Mansuri to demolish Tyre's citadel.

The Mamluks' next target was Sidon where Tibald Gaudin had sailed with the Templars' treasury and where the order planned to make a stand. A month later a Mamluk army under Sanjar al-Shuja'i appeared. The Templars were too few to defend the city, so retreated to the Castle of the Sea on a small islet close to the coast. Tibald sailed for Cyprus to get reinforcements but apparently despaired, and did nothing. When the Mamluks constructed causeways from the shore to the island the

The ruined church of one of the Carmelite monasteries on the southern side of Mount Carmel. (Author's photograph)

Crusader (Latin) military and diplomatic movements
1. Templars, Hospitallers and Order of St Thomas re-establish headquarters in Cyprus (1291).
2. Teutonic Knights re-establish headquarters in Venice (1291).
3. Order of St Lazarus re-establishes headquarters in Boigny (1291).
4. Garrisons of the remaining Crusader enclaves retreat to Cyprus
5. Much of the Crusader States aristocracy settles in Cyprus or in Crusader Greece (1291).
6. Pope Nicholas IV dies (1291).
7. Charles II of southern Italy, proposes alliance with the Despot Nicephorus of Epirus (1291).
8. Genoa sends a fleet to support the Byzantine Emperor's attack on Arta (1291).
9. King Henry II sends a fleet to raid Alexandria (1292).
10. Some captives from the fall of Acre are released up to ten years later.
11. A Templar garrison holds the small off-shore island of Arwad until expelled by the Mamluks (1302).
12. Peter Embriaco retains control of Gibelet (until at least 1302).
13. Hospitallers conquer Byzantine (1309).
14. Teutonic Knights relocate their headquarters in Marienburg (1309).
15. Travellers to Egypt and Syria report Islamic converts from military orders after fall of Acre.
16. Much of the poorer population of the final Crusader enclaves remains after the Mamluk conquest.

Mamluk military movements
17. Sultan Khalil sends forces to take remaining Crusader-held coastal enclaves (May–August 1291).
18. Khalil orders razing of Acre's fortifications (1291–92).
19. Abbasid Caliph proclaims *jihad* against Mongol Il-Khans (early 1292).
20. Sultan Khalil attacks fortress of Qal'at al-Rum (May 1292).
21. A Mamluk army ambushed by rebels north-east of Beirut (1292).
22. Sultan Khalil assassinated by senior amirs (13 December 1293).

Il-Khan diplomatic and political movements
23. Il-Khan embassy remains in Rome after death of Khan Arghun and fall of Acre.
24. Gaihatu is elected as new Il-Khan (22 June 1291)

Other Christian military movements
25. Byzantine Emperor Andronicus II invades the Despotate of Epirus and, with the held of a Genoese fleet, attacks its capital of Arta (1291).

Templars sailed to Tartus on 14 July. Prior to that, however, the evacuation of civilians to Cyprus had been completed.

Sixteen days later Haifa surrendered without resistance, the monasteries on Mount Carmel being destroyed. Next came Beirut, which surrendered to Shuja'i on 31 July, the defenders having sailed to Cyprus with various relics from the Cathedral. On 3 August, Tartus was evacuated after a brief siege, followed on 14 August by the castle of Atlit which the Templars simply abandoned.

Carrier pigeons took news of the taking of Acre to Damascus on the day it fell. Sultan Khalil himself left on 7 June and on his arrival in Damascus, according to Ibn Taghribirdi:

The entire city had been decorated, and sheets of satin had been laid along his triumphal path through the city leading to the palace of the naib (governor). The regal Sultan was preceded by 280 fettered prisoners. One bore a reversed Frankish banner, another carried a banner and spear from which the hair of slain

87

The Templar castle of Atlit was almost invulnerable to Mamluk siege as long as Christian shipping dominated the eastern Mediterranean. However, its garrison was so small that the castle was abandoned less than three months after the fall of Acre. (Author's photograph)

comrades were suspended. (Sultan) Al-Ashraf was greeted by the whole population of Damascus and the surrounding countryside lining the route, ulama, mosque officials, sufi shaykhs, Christians, and Jews, all holding candles even though the parade took place before noon.

Sultan Khalil subsequently returned to Egypt where he gave thanks for his victory at his father's tomb. Meanwhile Cairo was even more elaborately decorated than Damascus, including miniature fortresses which took forty days to erect along the parade route.

Acre was virtually abandoned and about ten years later al-Dimashqi wrote; 'At the present day Acre is in ruins…. and I myself was present at its capture, and had booty there.' Loot made some people very rich and, according to al-Yusufi, 'A certain Siraj al-Din Tibyan gained about 1,600 dinars and 22,000 dirhams and needed three rows of porters to carry his loot to Cairo.' Sanjar al-Shuja'i took an almost archaeological interest in the demolition of Acre, sending a carved stone plaque with Greek or Latin inscriptions dated AD222 to Damascus to be translated. It supposedly predicted the appearance of an Arab prophet who would conquer the world! Perhaps Sanjar, though highly educated, was taken for a ride like so many souvenir-hunting tourists in later years. The doorway of the Church of St Andrew was taken to Cairo, where it was added to the mausoleum of Sultan Qalawun.

From Sidon northwards, many ex-Crusader fortifications along the steep and mountainous coast were repaired and garrisoned by the Mamluks. South of Sidon their defensive policy was different. Here, on the largely low-lying coast of Palestine and along northern Sinai, fortifications were destroyed so that they could not provide bases for any future Crusades. Instead the region was defended by mobile forces based further inland. Beyond Sinai the Nile Delta coast was again strongly defended by fortified and garrisoned cities supported by the main Mamluk army in Cairo.

According to the Italian chronicler De Neocastro, a Greek monk named Arsenius brought the news to the Pope in Rome, with the words: 'Holy Father, if you have not heard about our sorrow, out of the bitterness of my heart I will reveal it. Would to God you had not been so intent on recovering Sicily (from the Aragonese)!' Pope Nicholas IV died in autumn 1291, never having recovered from the shock of Acre. Far away in Iran, the Il-Khan ruler Arghun had already died, his successor Gaihatu being elected on 22 July 1291.

The search for those to blame for Christendom's humiliation started immediately, and continued for centuries. However, some church and lay thinkers were already looking at the relationship between Christianity and Islam in a different way. Sadly they always remained a minority. This more tolerant attitude was summed up by the Dominican friar Ricoldo who reached Baghdad a few years after the fall of Acre. Around 1294 he wrote:

> *Who will not be astonished if he carefully considers how great is the concern of these very Muslims for study, their devotion in prayer, their pity for the poor, their reverence for the name of God and the prophets and the holy places, their sobriety in manners, their hospitality to strangers, their harmony and love for each other?*

Some other people now questioned the very reason for the existence of the Military Orders. Their prestige had suffered a massive blow, and although the Hospitallers and Teutonic Knights would eventually recover, the Templars never did. Most shocking in the eyes of ordinary people had been the competition between these Orders. Various ways of dealing with such shortcomings were suggested, including sending each Order to a different front, or combining them into one great Order.

While Europe was shocked by the fall of Acre, the opposite was true in the Islamic world and many panegyrics were penned praising the Mamluk Sultan. Shaykh al-Munji wrote: 'You have not left the miscreants a single town in which to hide,' while the *qadi* Abu'l-Tana declared: 'God is pleased! The Kingdom of the Cross has perished. After the destruction of the walls of Acre, the Infidelity (across the seas) will have nothing to find along our coasts.' Other poets addressed the defeated enemy; 'Oh you yellow-faced Christians, the vengeance of God has come down upon you. Oh you images which decorate churches, too long have proud chieftains been seen prostrating themselves before you.' There were also widespread efforts to equate the achievements of Sultan al-Ashraf Khalil with those of Saladin. An inscription in the citadel of Baalbek, carved two months after the fall of Acre, announced that al-Ashraf was: 'The probity of this world and religion… the subjugator of the worshippers of crosses, the conqueror of the coastal marches, the reviver of the 'Abbasid state.'

Western historians tend to see the fall of Acre in 1291 as the final chapter in Islam's struggle against the Crusaders, but many Muslim chroniclers regarded it as just one episode in a longer *jihad* against numerous foes of whom the most dangerous, the Mongols, still remained. Certainly Sultan Khalil wanted to turn the current enthusiasm and confidence against the Il-Khans. Three months after the taking of Acre, he persuaded the 'Abbasid Khalif – who lived as a Mamluk puppet in Cairo – to proclaim a *jihad* against the Mongols. Preachers picked up the theme and, according to al-Jazari, 'In Damascus they made great iron chains for the bridge to carry the troops to

Baghdad (across the Euphrates) which they hung up in the Great Mosque of Damascus to intimidate the enemy.'

The Il-Khans were such a powerful foe that careful preparations had to be made. A campaign led by Baydara al-Mansuri against autonomous *jabaliyun* hill peoples in the Lebanese mountains in 1292 was, however, ambushed and defeated. Sultan Khalil also sent an ironic message to the King of Cilician Armenia with condolences for the recent Christian catastrophe at Acre. In May 1292 the Sultan Khalil followed this up with a successful attack on the Armenian fortress of Qal'at al-Rum. This was proclaimed as the start of a greater war against the Mongols which would supposedly liberate the Jazira, Anatolia, Iraq and even parts of Iran. Meanwhile, the arrest of Muhammad Husam al-Din, leader of the powerful Mira bedouin tribe and Lord of Tudmur (Palmyra), in 1293 may have formed part of these political and military preparations. However, a second campaign against Cilicia in 1293 was called off when the Armenians surrendered several castles

Husam al-Din Lajin had been released following the fall of Acre, but later in 1292 he was arrested again, this time for being suspiciously close to Rukn al-Din Taqsu whom Sultan Khalil accused of treason. This time Lajin was saved by the intercession of Baydara al-Mansuri, though five of his supposed co-conspirators were strangled. Sultan Khalil's ever expanding ambitions clearly worried his more realistic officers. Eventually a group of *amirs* decided that he had become a threat to the Mamluk state and on 13 December 1293 al-Ashraf Khalil, the conqueror of Acre, was assassinated in a coup led by Baydara al-Mansuri. In fact Khalil made several mistakes, even before getting carried away with his own military power. As the Circassian *mamluks*, recruited by Khalil to balance the power of his father's Turkish *mamluks*, rose up the ranks, the Turks feared for their positions. Khalil's choice of Ibn al-Sal'us, an Arab ex-merchant rather than a *mamluk* warrior, as his closest confidant and *wazir* worried the Turks still further. Worse still, the new wazir was arrogant towards the Mamluk *amirs*, particularly towards the vice-regent Baydara.

The anonymous Templar of Tyre, now apparently living in Cyprus, included a garbled account of the coup in his chronicle but, given his normally excellent sources of information, this version might include elements of truth:

> It happened that one day as he was out on a hunt, they fell upon him and slew him. The one who struck the first blow was Baydara, who was his uncle, his mother's brother. He struck so half-heartedly that he did not cause a mortal wound. Thereupon an amir named Lajin, Sultan Khalil's sword-bearer and later a Sultan himself, struck him, saying to Baydara, "You do not strike like a man who wants to be sultan! But I will give him a manly blow," and he hacked him so that he cut him in two. Thus was Christianity avenged of the wrongs which he (Sultan Khalil) had committed.

Ironically, the last surviving top-ranking *amir* of the Salihi regiment recruited by the last effective Ayyubid ruler of Egypt, al-Salih (ruled 1240–49), died peacefully in his bed in 1306. His name was Bektash al-Fakhri and if he was the same Badr al-Din Bektash al-Fakhri whom the Templar Grand Master regarded as his best spy from within the Mamluk officer corps, then he may have been amongst the most effective double-agents in history.

The Crusades had been a disaster for the indigenous Christian communities of the Middle East; the later 13th and early 14th centuries seeing a steep decline in their status and numbers. Even in Cilicia, where the Armenian kingdom survived for many more years, morale slumped and Marco Polo, who visited the area in 1296, wrote that the people who had once been worth five warriors from any other nation were now 'slavish men given to gluttony and drinking'. In Lebanon three Mamluk punitive campaigns almost wiped out the Christian and Shia populations of the Kisrawan region. In cities like Damascus the educated Muslim élites steadily replaced the Christians who had traditionally provided the upper ranks of the civilian bureaucracy. The Jews suffered less, since they had been neither pro-Crusader nor pro-Mongol. In Egypt, the previous trickle of Coptic conversion to Islam now became a flood, even in the south where Christian Copts had until now formed a majority. Their close links with the African Christians of what are now Sudan and Ethiopia were similarly weakened as the Christian kingdoms of Nubia declined.

Mamluk campaigns to control what had been the almost autonomous regions of southern Egypt resulted in large numbers of Muslim Arab bedouin fleeing into the Sudan where they clashed with the Arab-Nubian Banu Kanz and the Nubian kingdoms. Other Mamluk armies followed during the early 14th century, accelerating the decline of both Makuria and Alwa until, by the end of the medieval period, Sudanese Christianity had disappeared. Christian Ethiopia survived, of course, as it does today, but another Christian community which no longer exists was that on the great island of Socotra, off the coast of Somalia, though they were mentioned by a group of Dominican missionary friars before 1315.

THE BATTLEFIELDS TODAY

The campaigns of Sultan Qalawun and Sultan Khalil from 1286 to 1291 covered an immense area, some of which has already been described in previous books in this series (see Campaign 19: *Hattin 1187*, and Campaign 132: *The First Crusade 1096–99*).

Tripoli is the biggest city in northern Lebanon, is easy to reach and has plenty of hotels and restaurants. Unfortunately it also has an exceptionally humid summer climate. Car-hire is also easy in Lebanon, though rather expensive, and travellers should book well ahead as this country is popular with high-spending regional visitors, especially from the Gulf States and Saudi Arabia. The best alternative is travel by the air-conditioned, frequent, reasonably priced and modern buses which link all towns. Travel by taxi is expensive but there are always the cheap, cheerful and extremely frequent mini-buses for those willing to go downmarket. Mini-buses also enable visitors to meet local people.

The coastal region of Lebanon formed the bulk of what little territory the Crusader States still controlled in 1286. It is dotted with medieval towns and citadels, all of which can be reached along the main coastal road. Even the deep south, next to the Israeli frontier, is now open to visitors, though the frontier itself remains closed at the time of writing. The beautiful mountains of Lebanon provided timber for Mamluk mangonels. East of these mountains, in the Beqaa valley, lies the magnificent town of Baalbek, whose citadel is best known for its Roman temples. Yet it also served as a vital Mamluk frontier fortress and contains impressive examples of medieval Islamic military architecture.

Those travelling from Tripoli into Syria along the fertile Buqa'ia valley to the ancient inland cities of Hims, Hama and then Damascus will pass through an astonishing variety of landscapes, if necessary within a single day. Anyone taking this route is, however, strongly advised not to rush. Whereas Hims is not particularly picturesque, it contains a number of interesting medieval Islamic buildings. A short distance north lies Hama, which certainly is picturesque with its creaking waterwheels, tumbling river, beautiful mosques and fine outdoor restaurants. Battlefield explorers with extra time might be interested in seeing the rarely visited region east of Hama and Hims. Green for part of the year, but dried to a crisp in summer and fading into semi-desert then true desert as one travels eastward, this landscape formed the heartland of Syria's original Arab population and they are still fiercely proud of their bedouin ancestry.

South of Hims the modern multi-lane highway to Damascus steadily climbs into a drier and bleaker landscape until it crosses a range of small mountains which lie in the rain-shadow of the higher Anti-Lebanon range which is itself in the shadow of massive Mount Lebanon. To get an idea of the extraordinary difficulties which troops taking the great mangonels to

Damascus had to face one should turn off the main road, up into the foothills of the Anti-Lebanon. Better still, do this in winter! Damascus itself is a thriving modern capital with all the facilities which visitors could require, whatever their price range. It is also one of the most fascinating medieval cities in the Middle East, rivalling even Cairo and Istanbul.

Acre is the most beautiful city in Israel – assuming that one does not accept Israel's self-declared annexation of the Old City of Jerusalem. It also has the advantage of retaining an Palestinian Arab population who are still a majority within the old city's fortifications. Once again there is a full range of accommodation, from Youth Hostels to multi-star hotels, while the restaurants are even better – especially those next to the harbour. The modern suburbs of Acre cover what was once the fortified Crusader suburb of Montmusard as well as the Mamluk siege lines, though the ancient Tal al-Fukhar, where Sultan Khalil and Napoleon Bonaparte both sited their headquarters, remains an open area. Southward along the Bay of Acre, a grim industrial zone spreads to the north-eastern outskirts of Haifa – itself one of the most pleasant, if not particularly historic, cities in Israel. The coastline north of Acre to the Lebanese frontier is much less spoiled.

Those wanting to visit the other area where Mamluk armies campaigned during these years will need to be prepared for some 'real' travel. Nubia has not, as is so often believed, been drowned by the waters of Lake Nasser. What has disappeared is the northernmost frontier region of medieval Makuria, and even here part of the forbidding 'Belly of Stones' remains south of the man-made lake. Ferries sail from Aswan to Wadi Halfa on the northern frontier of Sudan, after which a railway and a road cut across the desert to rejoin the great S-bend of the Nile at Abu Hamed before heading south to Khartoum. The heartland of medieval Christian Makuria lay along the southern part of the Nile's great curve, with its capital at what is now called Old Dongola and this region is more easily reached from Atbara or Khartoum rather than Abu Hamed or Wadi Halfa. Within Nubia the most enjoyable means of transport is by ferry along the river Nile. Otherwise there are buses, mini-buses and, where no real roads exist, lorries which carry people as well as goods and animals.

FURTHER READING

Abu'l-Fida (tr. P.M. Holt), *The Memoires of a Syrian Prince; Abu'l Fida, Sultan of Hamah (672-737/1273-1331)* (Wiesbaden, 1983)

Amitai, R., 'Foot Soldiers, Militiamen and Volunteers in the Early Mamluk Army,' in F.R. Chase (ed.), *Texts, Documents and Artefacts. Islamic Studies in Honour of D.S. Richards* (Leiden, 2003) pp.233–49

Anon. (ed.), *Acri 1291 – la fine della prezenza degli ordini militari in Terra Santa.... a cura di Francesco Tommasi (Biblioteca di Militia Sacra 1)* (Perugia, 1996)

Anonymous Mamluk *jundi* soldier, in Zetterstéen, K.V. (ed. & tr.), *Beiträge zur Geschichte der Mamlükensultaner* (Leiden, 1919) pp.2–3

Ayalon, D., *Islam and the Abode of War: Military Slaves and the Adversaries of Islam* (London, 1994); collected articles

Ayalon, D., *Studies in the Mamluks of Egypt* (London, 1977); collected articles

Ayalon, D., *The Mamluk Military Society* (London, 1979); collected articles

Balard, M., 'Les formes militaires de la colonisation génoise (XIIIe-XVe siècles),' in A. Bazzana (ed.), *Castrum III* (Madrid, 1988) pp.67–78

Byrne, E.H., 'The Genoese Colonies in Syria,' in L.J. Paetow (ed.), *The Crusades and Other Historical Essays Presented to Dana C. Monro by his Former Students* (New York, 1928) pp.139–82

Chamberlain, M., *Knowledge and Social Practice in Medieval Damascus, 1190–1350* (Cambridge, 1994)

Chevedden, P.E., 'Fortifications and the Development of Defensive Planning in the Latin East,' in D. Kagay & L.J.A. Villalon (eds.), *The Circle of War in the Middle Ages* (Woodbridge, 1999) pp.33–43

Claverie, P.-V., 'La contribution des templiers de Catalogne à la defense de la Syria Franque (1290–1310),' U. Vermeulen (ed.), *Egypt and Syria in the Fatimid, Ayyubid and Mamluk Eras, vol. 3, Proceedings of the 6th, 7th and 8th International Colloquium* (Leuven, 2001) pp.171–92

Clifford, E.R., *A Knight of Great Renown, The Life and Times of Othon de Grandson* (Chicago, 1961)

Crawford, P. (tr.), *The 'Templar of Tyre': Part III of the 'Deeds of the Cypriots'* (Aldershot, 2003)

Cuoq, J., *Islamisation de la Nubie Chretienne VIIe-XVIe Siècles* (Paris 1986)

Edbury, P.W., *The Kingdom of Cyprus and the Crusades 1191–1374* (Cambridge 1991)

Favreau-Lilie, M.-L., 'The Military Orders and the Escape of the Christian Population from the Holy Land in 1291,' *Journal of Medieval History* XIX (1993) pp.201–227

Favreau-Lilie, M.-L., 'The Teutonic Knights in Acre after the fall of Montfort (1271): Some Reflections,' in B.Z. Kedar (ed.), *Outremer: Studies in the History of the Crusading Kingdom of Jerusalem* (Jerusalem, 1982) pp.272–84

Forey, A., *The Military Orders from the Twelfth to the Early Fourteenth Centuries* (London, 1992)

Hamilton, B., 'Our Lady of Saidnaiya: an Orthodox shrine revered by Muslims and Knights Templar at the time of the Crusades,' in R.N. Swanson (ed.), *The Holy Land, Holy Lands, and Christian History* (Woodbridge, 2000) pp.207–15

Hitti, P.K., 'The Impact of the Crusades on Eastern Christianity,' in S.A. Hanna (ed.), *Medieval and Middle Eastern Studies in Honor of Aziz Suryal Atiya* (Leiden, 1972) pp.211–17

Holt, P.M., 'Mamluk–Frankish diplomatic relations in the reign of Qala'un...' *Journal of the Royal Asiatic Society* (1989) pp.278–89

Holt, P.M., *Early Mamluk Diplomacy (1260–1290): Treaties of Baybars and Qalaun and the Crusaders* (Leiden, 1995)

Housley, N., 'Charles II of Naples and the Kingdom of Jerusalem,' *Byzantion* 54 (1984) pp.527–535

Housley, N., *The Later Crusades, 1274–1580: From Lyons to Alcazar* (Oxford, 1992)

Humphreys, R.S., 'Ayyubids, Mamluks and the Latin East in the thirteenth century,' *Mamluk Studies Review* II (1998) pp.1–18

Humphreys, R.S., 'The Emergence of the Mamluk Army,' *Studia Islamica* XLV (1977) pp.67–99 & 147–82

Huygens, R.B.C. (ed.), *The Fall of Acre 1291* (Turnhout 2004); Master Thadeus, 'Ystoria de Desolatione et Concvlcatione Civitatis Acconensis et Tocins Terre Sancte' & Anon., 'Excidii Aconis Gestorvm Collectio.'

Ibn al-Suqa'i (ed. and tr. J. Sublet), *Tali Kitab Wafayat al-A'yan: Un fonctionaire chrétien dans l'administration mamelouke* (Damascus, 1974); biographical dictionary of the 13th century

Irwin, R., 'The Mamluk Conquest of the County of Tripoli,' in P.W. Edbury (ed.), *Crusade and Settlement* (Cardiff, 1985) pp.246–50

Irwin, R., *The Middle East in the Middle Ages: The Early Mamluk Sultanate 1250–1382* (London, 1986)

Jacoby, D., 'Les communes italiennes et les ordres militaires à Acre,' in M. Balard (ed.), *Etat et colonisations au Moyen Age et à la Renaissance* (Rheims, 1988) pp.193–214

Jacoby, D., *Recherches sur la Mediterranée Orientale du XIIe au XVe Siècle* (London, 1979)

Jacoby, D., *Studies on the Crusader States and on Venetian Expansion* (London, 1989); collected articles

Jacoby, D., *Trade. Commodities and Shipping in the Medieval Mediterranean* (London, 1997); collected articles

Kedar, B.Z., 'The Outer Walls of Frankish Acre,' in *'Atiqot XXXI* (1997) pp.157–80

Kingsford, C.L., 'Sir Otho de Grandson, 1238?–1328,' in *Transactions of the Royal Historical Society* 3 ser. III (1909) pp.125–95

Li Guo, *Early Mamluk Syrian Historiography: Al-Yunani's Dhayl Mir'at al-zaman* (Leiden, 1998)

Little, D.P., 'The Fall of 'Akk'a 690/1291: the Muslim version' in M. Sharon (ed.), *Studies in Islamic History and Civilization in Honour of Professor David Ayalon* (Leiden, 1986) pp.159–81

Lyons, U., and M.C. Lyons (tr.), *Ayyubids, Mamluks and Crusaders: Selections from the Tarikh al-Duwal wa'l-Muluk of Ibn al-Furat* (Cambridge, 1971)

Marshall, C.J., 'The French Regiment in the Latin East, 1254–91,' in *Journal of Medieval History* XV (1989) pp.301–07

Marshall, C.J., *Warfare in the Latin East, 1192–1291* (Cambridge, 1992)

Prawer, J., 'Military Orders and Crusader politics in the second half of the XIIIth century,' in J. Fleckenstein and M. Hellmann (eds.), *Die geistlichen Ritterorden Europas* (Sigmaringen, 1980) pp.217–29

Quatremere, E. (tr.), *Histoire des Sultans mamlouks de l'Egypte* (part of al-Maqrizi, *Kitab al-Suluk*) (Paris, 1837–45) 2 vols, 4 parts

Richard, J., 'Les Premiers missionaires latins en Ethiopie (XIIe-XIVe siècles),' in *Atti del Convegno di Studi Etiopici* (Rome, 1960) pp.323–29

Röhricht, R., 'Lettres de Ricoldo de Monte-Croce sur la prise d'Acre (1291),' in *Archives de l'Orient Latin II* (Paris, 1881; reprint 1964) pp.258–96

Sarraf, S. al-, 'Furusiyya Literature of the Mamluk Period,' in D. Alexander (ed.), *Furusiyya, volume 1. The Horse in the Art of the Near East* (Riyadh, 1996) pp.118–35

Sivan, E., *L'Islam et la Croisade: Idéologie et Propagande dans les Réactions Musulmanes aux Croisades* (Paris, 1968)

Stickel, E., *Der Fall von Akkon: Untersuchungen zum Abklingen des Kreuzzugsgedankens am Ende des 13. Jahrhunderts* (Bern & Frankfurt, 1975)

Yunini, Qutb al-Din al-, (ed. and tr. A. Melkonian), *Die Jahre 1287–1291 in der Chronik al-Yuninis (Dhayl Mir'at al-Zaman)* (Frieburg, 1975)

Ziadeh, N.A., *Urban Life in Syria under the Early Mamluks* (Westport, 1953)

INDEX

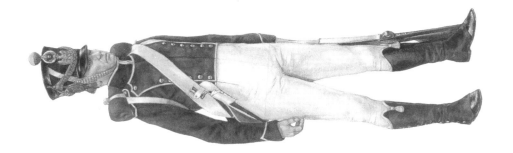

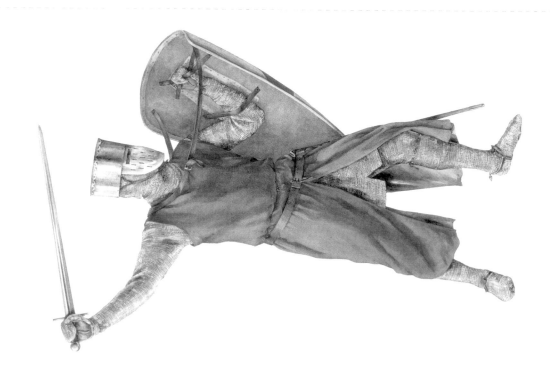

OSPREY
PUBLISHING

www.ospreypublishing.com

call our telephone hotline
for a free information pack

USA & Canada: 1-800-826-6600
UK, Europe and rest of world call:
+44 (0) 1933 443 863

Young Guardsman
Figure taken from *Warrior 22:*
Imperial Guardsman 1799–1815
Published by Osprey
Illustrated by Richard Hook

Knight, c.1190
Figure taken from *Warrior 1: Norman Knight 950 – 1204 AD*
Published by Osprey
Illustrated by Christa Hook

POSTCARD